Understanding Android Tablets and Smartphones For All Ages

Jim Gatenby

BERNARD BABANI (publishing) LTD
The Grampians
Shepherds Bush Road
London W6 7NF
England

www.babanibooks.com

Please Note

Although every care has been taken with the production of this book to ensure that all information is correct at the time of writing and that any projects, designs, modifications and/or programs, etc., contained herewith, operate in a correct and safe manner and also that any components specified are normally available in Great Britain, the Publishers and Author do not accept responsibility in any way for the failure (including fault in design) of any project, design, modification or program to work correctly or to cause damage to any equipment that it may be connected to or used in conjunction with, or in respect of any other damage or injury that may be so caused, nor do the Publishers accept responsibility in any way for the failure to obtain specified components.

Notice is also given that if equipment that is still under warranty is modified in any way or used or connected with home-built equipment then that warranty may be void.

© 2016 BERNARD BABANI (publishing) LTD

First Published – April 2016

British Library Cataloguing in Publication Data:

A catalogue record for this book is available from the British Library

ISBN 978-0-85934-763-1

Cover Design by Gregor Arthur

Printed and bound in Great Britain for Bernard Babani (publishing) Ltd

About This Book

The Android operating system (OS) controls most of the world's tablet computers and smartphones. Some manufacturers modify Android to suit their own needs but even these "tweaked" versions still have much in common with the standard Android.

This book has been prepared using a range of Android tablets and smartphones. These include standard Androids and also the Samsung Galaxy range with the TouchWiz user interface.

The first chapter gives an overview of the Android family and the essential technical terms, followed by setting up a new tablet, connecting to the Internet and creating a Google account. Exploring the various screens and personalising them is then covered, including downloading and installing *apps* from the Play Store. Later chapters describe browsing the Web, using text and voice searches. Using the Google Play Books app is then discussed, followed by YouTube, music, video and live and catchup television. Social networking including e-mail, Skype, Facebook, Twitter, WhatsApp and Instagram are also covered.

Chapter 8 describes the use of free software from the "clouds", including the Google Docs word processor and spreadsheet and the new Microsoft Word and Excel apps for Android. Also saving your files in the clouds and *syncing* to your other computers. Various methods of printing from Android smartphones and tablets both locally and remotely are also covered.

Managing your Android by connecting it to a PC or using a file manager app is discussed, together with connecting external devices such as flash drives, SD cards and Micro SD cards. The built-in cameras are also described. Essential security precautions are discussed.

The last chapter includes specialist applications such as using a smartphone as a *mobile hotspot* to connect a Wi-Fi only tablet to the Interrnet. Also covered is the use of an Android device as a *Sat Nav* and as a *QR barcode* scanner.

Android Devices Covered in this Book

The material in this book is suitable for Android smartphones and tablets in general and has been prepared using the Jelly Bean, KitKat, Lollipop and Marshmallow versions of the Android operating system. There are three basic Android device configurations to which this book applies:

- Wi-Fi Only Tablet
- 3G/4G Tablet
- Smartphone

Android 9 inch Wi-Fi tablet

Android 4.5 inch smartphone

The Wi-Fi Only Tablet

The Wi-Fi only tablet is a small hand-held computer, typically having a 9-10 inches screen measured diagonally. It has an on-screen keyboard and internal storage for saving files such as photos, documents, music, etc. It connects to the Internet through a Wi-Fi network such as a Wi-Fi router in the home or a public Wi-Fi access point or hotspot in a hotel, library or airport, etc. The Android tablet can access a store of over 2 million *apps* or programs for activities such as news, information, entertainment, work, maps and games. It cannot independently connect to a 3G/4G phone network.

The 3G/4G Tablet

This is basically the same as the Wi-Fi only tablet, but with the additional installation of a SIM card, as used on cell phones. This allows the tablet to connect to the Internet using a 3G or 4G cell phone network. Although relatively expensive, 3G/4G connectivity is useful in a situation where there is no Wi-Fi.

3G/4G Internet connectivity requires an account with a cell phone network such as EE, T-Mobile or Three and a *data plan* costing a monthly fee, allowing you to download a specified amount of data.

The new 3G/4G tablet costs more than the Wi-Fi only version of the same device. Although some 3G/4G tablets can be used as a mobile phone for dialling and receiving phone calls, most are used purely as a tablet for the vast range of Internet and other activities as discussed on the previous page. The larger size of the tablet makes it inconvenient to use as a mobile phone.

The Smartphone

This combines all the Internet and other functions of the Wi-Fi and 3G/4G tablets. In addition you can use the smartphone to send and receive SMS text messages and to make and receive phone calls, with a contacts list and dialling like a basic mobile phone.

Phone

SPEED DIAL	RECENTS	CONTACTS

A smartphone can also be used as a *mobile hotspot* to connect a Wi-Fi only tablet to the Internet via a 3G/4G network.

This book covers the main Internet and other computing uses of Wi-Fi only tablets, 3G/4G tablets and smartphones. It does not cover in detail the relatively straightforward use of a smartphone to make ordinary telephone calls.

About the Author

Jim Gatenby trained as a Chartered Mechanical Engineer and initially worked at Rolls-Royce Ltd using computers in the analysis of jet engine performance. He obtained a Master of Philosophy degree in Mathematical Education by research at Loughborough University of Technology and taught mathematics and computing in school for many years before becoming a full-time author. His most recent teaching posts included Head of Computer Studies and Information Technology Coordinator. The author has written over forty books in the fields of educational computing and Microsoft Windows, including many of the titles in the highly successful "Older Generation" series from Bernard Babani (publishing) Ltd.

Trademarks

Android Google, Google Drive, Google Chrome, Gmail, Google Cloud Print and YouTube are trademarks or registered trademarks of Google, Inc. Microsoft Windows, Microsoft Word, Microsoft Publisher, Microsoft Excel and Skype are trademarks or registered trademarks of Microsoft Corporation. Facebook is a registered trade mark of Facebook, Inc. Twitter is a registered trademark of Twitter, Inc. WhatsApp is a trademark or registered trademark of WhatsApp, Inc. Instagram is trademark or registered trademark of Instagram, Inc. Amazon Kindle is a trademark or registered trademark of Amazon.com, Inc. HP Print Service Plugin and HP ePrint are trademarks or registered trademarks of HP, Inc. All other brand and product names used in this book are recognized as trademarks or registered trademarks, of their respective companies.

Acknowledgements

I would like to thank my wife Jill for her support during the preparation of this book and also Michael Babani for making the project possible.

Contents

3

Screens, Apps and Widgets

5

6

7

8

9

10

The Android Family

What is an Android?

To science fiction enthusiasts, an Android is a robot designed to look and behave like a human. In the world of tablet computers and smartphones, Android is the most popular *operating system*. Android is owned by Google Inc., famous for their Internet search engine and many other leading software products, as shown below.

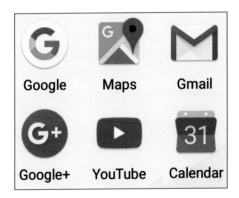

The Android Operating System

An *operating system* is a collection of *programs* or instructions which control all the basic functions of a computer, such as the screen display, running your chosen apps and saving your data.

The Android operating system is pre-installed on the Internal Storage of a new tablet or smartphone. Versions of Android are named after confectionery, such as Jelly Bean, KitKat, Lollipop and Marshmallow. Well over 90% of all Android tablets and smartphones use one of these versions of the operating system.

Android Apps

While the operating system controls the basic functions of the smartphone or tablet, you need software to perform the particular tasks you wish to do, such as sending an e-mail, playing music or reading an eBook, for example. The programs for your chosen activities are known as *apps*, the modern name for *application software*.

The Google Play Store

Android tablets and smartphones have access to over 2 million specially designed apps in the *Google Play Store*. These can be downloaded from the Internet and installed on your device.

Many of the apps are free or cost just a few pounds. Apps are available for a vast range of subjects such as Web browsing, free Skype worldwide video calls, Facebook, Twitter, WhatsApp and Instagram social networking, YouTube videos, music, live and catchup television, online newspapers, banking and games, etc.

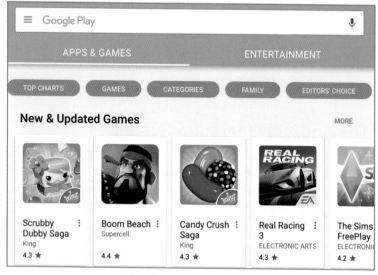

The Google Play Store

Android Tablets and Smartphones

Although the iPad and iPhone from Apple are extremely popular, they are outnumbered by Android devices. This is because lots of companies such as Google, Sony, Motorola and Samsung each produce a range of Android tablets and smartphones.

Smartphones vs Tablets

The smartphone is a mobile phone which also has all the functions of a tablet, such as browsing the Internet, e-mail, social networking, television and radio and a touchscreen *graphical user interface* (GUI).

Smartphones typically have a diagonal screen size of around 4 inches up to a maximum of 7 inches. Large smartphones with screen sizes above 5.5 inches are known as *phablets*.

Most Android tablets have a screen size of 7, 8, 9 or 10 inches. The Google Pixel C Android tablet has a screen size of 10.2 inches and an optional separate keyboard. Large tablets with a separate keyboard are also known as *hybrid* or *2-in-1* computers. These may be used like a laptop for more productive tasks, not just for entertainment or social networking, etc.

Relative sizes: tablet vs smartphone

More colourful Material Design screen used in Android Lollipop and Android Marshmallow

Nexus 9 tablet (8.9 ins)   **Moto G smartphone (4.5ins)**

The Android All Apps Screen

Android apps are launched by tapping icons on the Apps screen, using your finger or a *stylus*, a pen-like device with a rubber tip. Later versions of Android such as Lollipop and Marshmallow use the colourful *Material Design* interface shown below and on the previous page.

The Apps Screen: Standard Android

Earlier versions of Android such as KitKat and Jelly Bean use a very similar Apps screen. This is used in the same way but features a black background.

Samsung Galaxy Apps Screen

The Samsung Galaxy range, currently at version 7, is based on the standard Android operating system, but overlays some superficial screen designs known as the *TouchWiz* interface. These operate in much the same way as the standard Android OS described throughout this book.

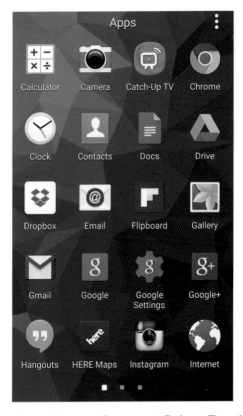

The Apps Screen: Samsung Galaxy TouchWiz

Some Popular Apps

Apps appear as icons on the All Apps screen, as shown on the previous page. Listed below are some very popular and useful Android apps, together with their icons.

The **Play Store** icon gives access to over 1.5 million apps in different categories. These are either free or can be bought online for a few pounds. When a new app is installed its icon appears on the Home and All Apps screens.

Google is a famous *search engine*. "To Google" means to search for information on a particular subject, after typing in some relevant *keywords*. Google also includes *voice search* for entering the keywords by speaking.

Google Chrome is a *web browser*, similar to Microsoft's Internet Explorer and Apple's Safari. A web browser is used to display web pages and to navigate between pages using *links*. You can also revisit web pages from your *browsing history* or which you've *bookmarked* for future viewing.

Google mail or **Gmail** is a free and popular e-mail service allowing you to send and receive messages consisting of text, pictures and attached files. Creating a Gmail account and password also gives you access to other Google services.

Google Earth allows you to zoom in and view different parts of the globe, using satellite images, aerial photography and images captured by cameras mounted on cars all over the world.

Play Books allows you to read books in your Library or download new ones from a choice of millions in the Play Store, some of them free.

YouTube is a free Google website which allows individuals and companies to upload and share videos for other people to view. These may include amusing incidents or popular music videos. If a video spreads quickly and is viewed by millions of people, it is said to "go viral".

Play Music allows you to shop for music to download to your tablet or smartphone or to play tracks already in your Library.

Play Movies & TV is used to download and watch videos and TV shows bought from the Play Store.

Facebook is the leading *social networking* website. Users of Facebook post their *Profile* or *Timeline* on the Internet, allowing them to become online *friends* with people of similar interests. Friends exchange news, information, photographs and videos, etc.

Twitter is a popular social networking website, on which users post short messages or *tweets* (up to 140 characters long). Celebrities use Twitter to air their views and may have thousands of followers. You can follow whoever you like, reply to *tweets*, or use Twitter for a campaign.

Skype allows you to make free worldwide Internet video and voice-only calls between all types of computer. The Skype app is free and Android devices generally have the necessary built-in microphone, speakers and cameras.

WhatsApp is a messaging service for smartphones, which allows free phone calls across the Internet, rather than the cell phone network. You can send and receive messages, photos and videos and voice messages.

Instagram is designed to capture and edit photos and videos and share them with family and friends. You can also view photos and messages posted by other people from around the world.

Essential Hardware Terms

The following list describes the main components in Android tablets and smartphones. The first three are present in some form in all types of computer — tablet, laptop and desktop, etc.

Processor

This is a chip which carries out all of the instructions and calculations involved in the execution of the current app or program. The speed of a processor is the rate at which it carries out instructions and is measured in GHz (Gigahertz). Typical processor speeds are between 1GHz and 2.5GHz.

Memory or RAM

This is the temporary store into which the instructions for the current program are loaded. The memory is cleared when the device is switched off. A shortage of memory causes a computer to run slowly. Typical Android memory sizes are 1GB-4GB (Gigabytes), similar to many laptop and desktop computers.

Internal Storage

This is not to be confused with the volatile, i.e. temporary, memory or RAM described above. The Internal Storage in a tablet or smartphone is a location where apps and data files such as photos and music can be permanently saved. The Internal Storage on a tablet or smartphone usually takes the form of an *SSD* (Solid State Drive). This has no moving parts, in contrast to the *hard disc drive* on a laptop or desktop computer, which consists of a number of magnetic discs rotating at high speed.

Apps and data files, such as eBooks, which are permanently saved on the Internal Storage, can be accessed offline, i.e. when not connected to the Internet. Typical Internal Storage sizes on a tablet or phone are 8GB, 16GB, 32GB and 64GB, compared with 500GB to 1000GB or 1TB (Terabyte) common on laptop and desktop computers. The Android device compensates for this by saving much of its data in the *clouds* on the Internet.

SD Card Slot

Some tablets and phones have a slot for a *Micro SD card*, similar to the SD (Secure Digital) cards used in cameras. This is used to supplement the Internal Storage of the tablet or phone. Typical Micro SD card capacities are 8GB, 16GB, 32GB, 64GB and 128GB. If you don't have a Micro SD slot you can connect a USB *SD card reader* via the Micro USB port, discussed below.

Micro USB Port

This is used for connecting a battery charger. It also allows you to connect a tablet or smartphone to a laptop or desktop machine for the transfer of files such as photos, music, videos or text documents. The Micro USB port can also be used to connect devices such as USB SD card readers, mice and keyboards.

Internet Connection

An Android device uses *Wi-Fi*, i.e. radio waves, to connect to the Internet usually via a *router* in your home or a Wi-Fi connection in a hotel or airport, etc. Some Androids have a slot for a 3G or 4G (3rd or 4th Generation) SIM card, providing connection to the Internet via one of the cell phone networks.

Cameras

A front webcam, facing the user, allows you to make video calls with Skype, etc. A rear camera, if available, allows you to take photos and videos in a similar way to a separate digital camera.

Micro HDMI Port

This allows an Android tablet to display photos and videos, etc., on a High Definition television, projector or computer monitor.

Screen Resolution

The resolution of the screen, usually measured in pixels or dots per inch, affects the sharpness and clarity of the display. The latest Google Pixel C has a resolution of 2560x1800 or 308 pixels per inch.

Typical Android Specifications

Shown below are the technical specifications of three popular Android devices. The Samsung Galaxy S7 Edge smartphone and the Google Pixel C are top-of-the-range devices costing around £400-£600.

Smartphones like the Samsung Galaxy S7 and S7 Edge are also available on contract from companies such as EE, Three, etc. Prices vary but may be around £30 -£50 per month for a two year contract.

The Hudl 2 has been a very popular budget tablet, selling for around £100 (or less for some Tesco customers), but unfortunately has been discontinued by the supermarket. Other budget tablets offering good performance, such as the Amazon Kindle Fire, are available for £50-£200.

	Samsung Galaxy S7 Edge	Google Pixel C	Tesco Hudl 2
Device type	Smartphone	Tablet	Tablet
Screen size	5.5ins	10.2ins	8.3ins
Android O.S.	Marshmallow	Marshmallow	Jelly Bean
Processor speed	2.3GHz	1.9GHz	1.83GHz
Internal storage	32/64GB	32GB/64GB	16GB
Memory (RAM)	4GB	3GB	2GB
Screen resolution	2560x1440 534ppi	2560x1800 308ppi	1920x1200 265ppi
Front camera **Rear camera**	4MP 12MP	2MP 8MP	1.2MP 5MP
Micro USB port	Yes	Yes	Yes
MicroSD card slot	Up to 200MB	—	32GB

Additional Information

Certain features were not included in the table on the previous page because they are normally provided as standard on all tablets and smartphones. For example, the 3.5mm audio jack or socket, which allows earphones or headphones to be connected.

Battery life between charges is important. Figures such as 10-12 hours are quoted, although this depends on what the device is being used for — Web browsing, watching videos, etc.

Prices of tablets and smartphones vary depending on the specification. For example, you may have a choice of 8GB, 16GB, 32GB or 64GB Internal Storage. If you want to save a lot of files on your Internal Storage, e.g. eBooks, music or videos for using *offline*, then you might prefer to pay for extra Internal Storage.

As shown in the table on the previous page, some devices have a slot for a *Micro SD* card, providing extra storage of perhaps 32GB, 64GB up to 200GB. If a device doesn't have a Micro SD slot, you can use the *Google Drive cloud storage* to store files, such as music, video, photos and documents, on the Internet. Alternatively, as discussed in detail later in this book, you can connect a *USB SD card reader* to the Micro USB battery charger port, standard on Android smartphones and tablets.

The Android operating system doesn't contain a *file manager* app, needed to copy files to and from a Micro SD card, but a free app is available from the Google Play Store, as discussed later

Some tablets may have an option, at an extra price, to provide 3G or 4G Internet connectivity via a mobile phone network. This allows you to connect to the Internet where there is no Wi-Fi.

The *Micro HDMI* port built into some devices can be used to connect a tablet or smartphone directly, via a single cable, to a High Definition television, projector or monitor. Devices without a Micro HDMI port can connect to an HD device via the micro USB port, using special cables and adaptors.

Androids Versus Laptops and Desktops

You could be forgiven for thinking a tiny smartphone or tablet could not possibly be as powerful as the much bigger laptop and desktop machines. As a regular user of all the hand-held devices, I have found that they are just as capable at browsing the Internet, playing music and videos, watching live and catchup TV, etc. Two of the critical factors which affect the power and performance of a computer are the processor speed and the amount of memory or RAM. In these two respects, the tablet or smartphone is just as well equipped as many laptop or desktop machines, with tablet processor speeds ranging from 1GHz to 2.5GHz and RAM sizes typically 1GB, 2GB, 3GB and 4GB. Other factors which have enabled the hand-held devices to seriously damage the sales of laptop and desktop machines are:

- The handy size of the tablet or smartphone means it can be carried in a small bag or largish pocket and easily used anywhere — in bed, on a train, in a café, etc.

- The tablet or phone doesn't need CDs and DVDs and associated drives for software. Thousands of apps and eBooks are available from the Play Store, many of them free.

- The Internal Storage (SSD) of the tablet or phone is much lighter than the hard disc drives in laptops and desktops. A large disc drive is not needed because your files can be saved *in the clouds*, as discussed later.

- The keyboard and other peripheral devices such as speakers, microphone, cameras, etc., are integral within the tablet. The tablet or phone doesn't need heavy duty cables and connecting ports, unlike the desktop machine.

- The tablet or phone has a small, light battery which can be used for about 10 hours — much longer than a typical laptop battery, while the desktop machine needs a mains power supply and a bulky built-in power supply unit.

Why Buy a Tablet or Smartphone?

Android smartphones and tablets are small, light, fast, inexpensive and easy to use. They are convenient to use anywhere, for very popular or useful activities such as:

- Getting the latest news and weather
- Sending and receiving e-mails and using Skype video calls and social networking
- Listening to music and watching videos, live and catch-up television
- Reading eBooks and online newspapers
- Browsing the Internet to find information on any subject — health, holidays, etc.
- Playing games
- Managing your bank account online
- Buying and selling anything online such as books, holidays, travel tickets

The Future

It's often said that the tablets and smartphones will spell the end for laptop and desktop machines. For the sort of activities listed above, the tablet is the first choice for many people. However, if you need to work for several hours at a desk producing long documents in an office, the laptop or desktop machine is probably the better option. Many people now regularly use all of the configurations — smartphones, tablets, laptop and desktop computers — for different tasks in different situations.

The *hybrid computer*, also known as the *2-in-1 computer*, i.e. a tablet with an attachable keyboard, can be used both as a tablet, e.g. for entertainment, information and communication and also as a laptop for productive work. In this context, extra large tablets are becoming available, aimed at business users.

2

Setting Up a New Tablet or Smartphone

Introduction

When you open the box containing a new Android tablet or smartphone, the only other contents are the cable and a special plug for charging the battery and perhaps a couple of flimsy instruction leaflets. As discussed in Chapter 1, the reason the tablet or phone can be so small is the absence of bulky peripheral devices such as disc drives, keyboards and cables, etc., needed by larger computers. This is possible because the Android can use *cloud storage* systems on the Internet, such as Google Drive and Dropbox. The clouds are also the main source of software or *apps* that you may want to download and install.

Charging the Battery

Although the battery may be partially charged on delivery, the instructions usually advise you to charge it further before you get started. One end of the charging cable plugs into the *Micro USB port* on the tablet or phone, as shown on the next page. The other end has a full-size USB connector which can be inserted into the special 3-pin 13-amp charger plug provided. Alternatively the tablet or phone can be charged by inserting the cable into a USB port on a laptop or desktop computer. This should be carried out with the device in sleep mode or switched off. Charging using a computer is slower than when the Android is connected to a charger plugged into a 13-amp socket.

An Android device lasts about 10 hours between charges, depending on the usage — music, browsing, videos, etc.

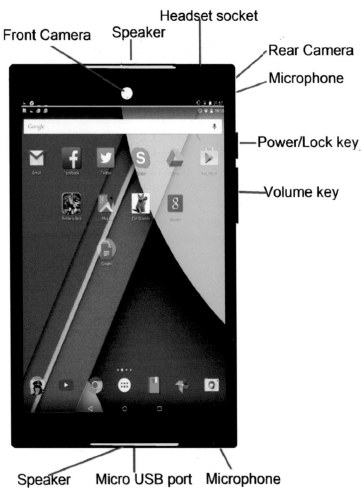

Front Camera   Speaker   Headset socket   Rear Camera   Microphone   Power/Lock key   Volume key   Speaker   Micro USB port   Microphone

The Android Tablet or Smartphone

The features above are broadly the same on all Android tablets and smartphones.

.

The Micro USB Port

This port, shown near the bottom of page 16, is standard on a new Android device and is primarily used to charge the battery. However, with the addition of a small *OTG* (On The Go) cable costing a few pounds, the Micro USB port can be converted to a full-size, standard USB port, compatible with a range of computing accessories such as a flash drive, SD card reader and a USB keyboard.

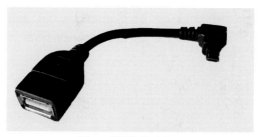

The OTG Cable

The Micro USB port can also be used to connect an Android tablet or smartphone to a laptop or desktop computer. The larger computer can then be used to manage the files on the Android, which doesn't have its own file manager software.

Please Note:

Later versions of the Android operating system such as Lollipop and Marshmallow use the more colourful Material Design interface, with light backgrounds to some features. Earlier versions of Android use slightly different screen designs, often including a black background. However, the methods of operating the various Android versions are basically the same. Where necessary, any differences are explained in the text.

Using the Touch Screen

- A single *tap* on an icon opens the app on the screen.

- Tap where you want to enter text and the *on-screen keyboard* pops up ready for you to start typing.

- *Tap and hold* displays a menu relevant to the current screen.

- *Touch and hold* an item such as an app or a widget, before dragging it to a new position with the finger.

- *Swipe* or *slide* a finger across the screen to scroll across Home Screens or unlock the Lock Screen.

- *Pinch* two fingers together to zoom out of a picture or map, etc., or *stretch* the fingers apart to zoom in.

Please Note:

- If you find it difficult to use a touch screen with your fingers, you might prefer using a *stylus,* as shown on page 20, for some of the above gestures.

- Instead of entering words using the on-screen keyboard, the Android has a very effective *voice recognition* system, discussed on page 21.

- As discussed in Chapter 9, if you need to do a lot of text entry, you can connect a separate keyboard, mouse and monitor.

The On-screen Keyboard

The on-screen keyboard, shown below, pops up whenever you tap in a slot intended for the entry of text.

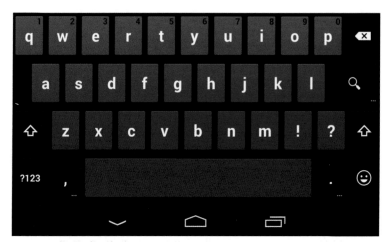

The on-screen keyboard: Android J & K

The three icons along the bottom of the on-screen keyboard shown above have the following functions.

 Hide the on-screen keyboard.

 Return to the Home screen, discussed in Chapter 3.

 Display recently visited pages in the form of thumbnail images.

The Android keyboard above includes a toggle key shown on the right to switch between either letters, as shown above, or a combination of numbers punctuation marks and symbols.. **?123**

The on-screen keyboard on later Android devices is broadly similar, apart from the colour scheme as shown below.

The on-screen keyboard: Android L & M

The three icons at the bottom are slightly different, as described below.

Hide the on-screen keyboard.

Return to the Home screen, discussed in Chapter 3.

Display recently visited pages in the form of a revolving *carousel*, as shown in Chapter 3, page 33.

The Stylus

If you find accurate typing difficult using the on-screen keyboard, a cheap *stylus*, (under £2) as shown on the right, may help.

Samsung Galaxy On-screen Keyboard

The keyboard for a Galaxy smartphone is shown below.

Instead of buttons at the bottom of the main screen area as shown on pages 19 and 20, the Galaxy range have the controls built into the bezel or frame of the device, as shown below.

The left-hand button above displays the carousel of previously visited apps, as shown on page 33. The middle button returns you to the central Home screen. The right-hand button displays the previously visited screen.

Voice or Speech Recognition

When entering text in an app such as Google Docs, as discussed in Chapter 8, the on-screen keyboard displays a microphone icon, as shown on the right and below.

Tap the microphone icon to open the *voice recognition* window, ready for you to start speaking the text into the word processor or e-mail app, etc.

As discussed later, when searching with Google, instead of typing the keywords for the search, tap the microphone icon or say "**Ok Google**". Then say the search keywords.

Starting Up: The Lock Screen

Hold down the Power/lock key, shown on page 16, for a few seconds until the *Lock Screen* appears as shown below.

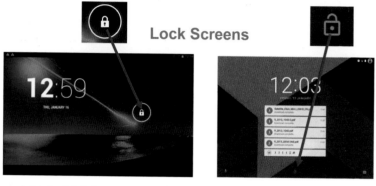

Lock Screens

Android J & M

Android L & M

Shown on the left above is the earlier Lock Screen used on Android Jelly Bean for example. Later Android versions such as Lollipop and Marshmallow use the Lock Screen shown on the right above. This later Lock Screen also shows *notifications*, i.e. short messages informing you, for example, that a file has been *downloaded* from the Internet and saved on your device.

Swipe the padlock icon shown above upwards to the right by touching it and sliding the finger across the screen. Swiping the Lock Screen opens the *Home screen*, discussed in Chapter 3. You are now ready to select the app for your chosen activity such as searching the Internet or watching a video, etc.

Samsung Galaxy

On the Samsung Galaxy simply swipe across the lock screen.

Security

Various more secure alternatives to swiping the Lock Screen are discussed in Chapter 9.

Connecting to Wi-Fi

A Wi-Fi connection is usually made via a *broadband router* in your home or in a hotel or café, etc. Broadband packages with an Internet Service Provider often include a router.

After selecting your language, the Android tablet or phone should automatically detect any available Wi-Fi networks as shown at the bottom of this page. Alternatively, open **SETTINGS** by tapping its icon, shown below, on the Apps screen.

 Settings icons

Jelly Bean   **Later Androids + Galaxy**

After tapping **Wi-Fi**, you should see a list of available networks. If necessary tap or slide the switch as shown below to set **Wi-Fi** as **ON**.

Earlier versions of Android use a black background in dialogue boxes, but otherwise they are basically the same technically.

The small padlock icon shown on the right next to the Wi-Fi icons, indicates a *secure network,* requiring a password to be entered before you can connect to it.

Tap the name of the router or network you wish to connect to. The on-screen keyboard, shown on page 19, 20 or 21, automatically pops up, enabling you to enter the password for the network, as shown below.

Locating the Password for a Router

The password can usually be found on the back of a home network router or from the staff of a hotel, etc.

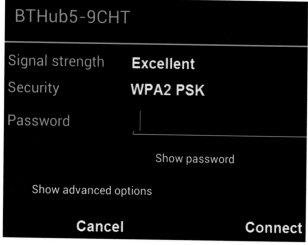

BTHub5-9CHT	
Signal strength	**Excellent**
Security	**WPA2 PSK**
Password	

Show password

Show advanced options

Cancel   **Connect**

Entering the router password

(Although the colour schemes vary, the window shown above for entering the password is similar on all versions of Android).

Tap **Connect**, shown above on the lower right to complete the process of getting online to the Internet.

Checking Your Wi-Fi Connection

You can check your Wi-Fi settings at any time by opening the main settings screen and selecting Wi-Fi as described on page 23. (You can also check your Wi-Fi in the **Quick Settings** panel as discussed on pages 27, 64 and 65). The word **Connected** should now appear below the selected Wi-Fi network, as shown below.

Tap on the name of the router to view the status and performance of your network. As shown below, the speed of the network is much less when the tablet or phone is further away from the router, especially in another room with walls in between.

BTHub5-9CHT	The effect of distance from the router	BTHub5-9CHT
Status **Connected**		Status **Connected**
Signal strength **Fair**		Signal strength **Excellent**
Link speed **26 Mbps**		Link speed **780 Mbps**
Frequency **2.4 GHz**		Frequency **5 GHz**
Security **WPA2 PSK**		Security **WPA2 PSK**
20 metres away		**1 metre away**

Creating a Gmail Account

If you haven't got a Gmail account with an e-mail address and password, you can create one during the initial setting up process for a new Android tablet or phone. It's worth opening a Gmail account because it gives access to several other free Google services, such as Google Drive cloud computing and also Google Docs office software. These topics are discussed later.

You can create a new Google account at any time by opening **SETTINGS**, as discussed on page 23. Then under **ACCOUNTS**, tap **+Add account**, then tap **Google**.

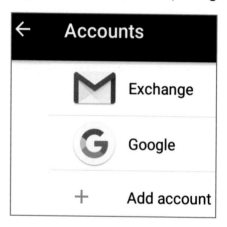

You are then required to enter your first and last name and choose your e-mail address such as:

jimsmith@gmail.com

If your chosen name has already been taken you may need to choose a different name or add some numbers, such as :

jimsmith77@gmail.com

As discussed later, a Google account with *Google Drive* allows you to access your photos and documents, etc., on any computer anywhere — Android, laptop or desktop PC.

Rotation of the Screen

The screen can be locked in the vertical or horizontal position or it can rotate automatically when you rotate the tablet or phone. To change the rotation setting in Jelly Bean and KitKat, swipe down from the top right of the screen to display the **Quick Settings** window. Then tap the **Auto-rotate** icon switch between **AUTO ROTATE** and **ROTATION LOCKED** settings.

In Lollipop and Marshmallow, the **Quick Settings** window is displayed by swiping down *twice* from the top of the screen. The **ROTATION LOCKED** setting is now known as **Portrait**.

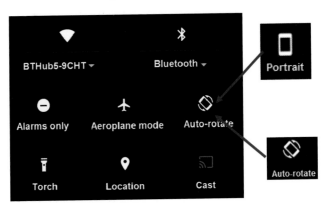

Samsung Galaxy

Swipe down from the top of the screen to display the small settings shown below. The green icons represent features that are switched **On**, such as **Screen rotation** shown below.

Checking the Battery

The right-hand side of the Status Bar at the top right of the screen, shown here on the right, gives a rough indication of the battery life and whether or not it's currently being charged. The other icons on the right above, show whether Wi-Fi and Aeroplane mode are switched on, followed on the right by the current time.

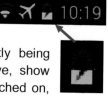

Alternatively, to see the remaining charge as a percentage, swipe down from the top right of the screen to display the **Quick Settings** window shown on page 27. (On Lolllipop and Marshmallow swipe down twice).

More detailed information about the battery can be found by opening the main **Settings** feature discussed on pages 23 and 68 and then selecting **Battery**.

Shutting Down

Hold down the Power/Lock key shown on page 16, until **Power Off** appears. Tap **Power off** followed by tapping **OK,** if necessary, to finish the shut down. On later devices simply tap **Power off**. The Samsung Galaxy displays a menu as shown on the right. For example, you can tap to enable **Flight mode**, as discussed elsewhere in this book.

Screens, Apps and Widgets

The Home Screens

Start the Android tablet or smartphone by holding down the Power button, shown on page16. Then swipe the padlock on the Lock Screen upwards to open the central *Home screen*, as shown below.

There are several Home screens on an Android tablet or smartphone. The central Home screen has a number of preinstalled apps and you can install more from the Play Store. You can move between the various Home screens by swiping left or right. You can also display Google Cards showing latest information, as discussed on page 54.

The Favorites Tray (or Screen Dock)

Along the bottom of all the Home screens is the *Favorites Tray* shown below, giving quick access to frequently used apps.

As discussed shortly, you can swap most of the icons on the Favorites Tray to give quick access to frequently used apps.

As shown above and on the right, there is a row of 5 dots just above the Favorites Tray. The example on the right shows that the central Home screen is selected.

The All Apps Icon

The *Apps* icon shown on the right and on the Favorites Tray above is a permanent fixture in the centre of the Favorites Tray. Tapping this icon opens the *Apps screen*, as shown on the next page. This displays all the apps installed on the smartphone or tablet.

Apps

Samsung Galaxy

The Samsung Galaxy uses the Apps icon shown on the right. This is also shown below on the TouchWiz *Shortcuts Bar*, which is similar to the standard Android Favorites Tray shown above.

Apps

The Apps Screens

In addition to the Home screens, there are several Apps screens. These contain a number of apps preinstalled on a new tablet or smartphone. In addition you can install further apps from the Google Play Store, as discussed shortly. Sample Apps screens are shown below.

Android J & K

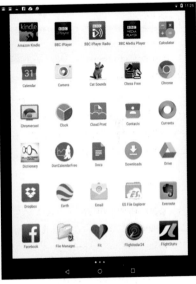

Android L & M

The Samsung Galaxy app screen is shown on page 5.

Icons can be copied from the Apps screens to blank spaces on your Home screens to make your own personal Home screens.

Changing the Background Colour of the Apps Screen

Some people have said they prefer the black background on the Apps screen to the new white background on Android Lollipop and Marshmallow, shown above on the right. The background can be changed using the free *Nova Launcher* app, together with other alternative settings, as discussed on page 47.

Navigating the Screens
Android J & K

The Navigation Bar shown below is used to switch between the different screens, in addition to the methods of swiping left or right or tapping the All Apps icon shown on page 30. The Navigation Bar appears along the bottom of all the Home screens.

Navigation Bar: Android J & K

- The left-hand button above opens the previous screen.
- The button in the middle opens the central Home screen.
- The right-hand button displays thumbnails of the recently visited apps, which can be scrolled horizontally.

Recent Apps: Android J & K

Tap a thumbnail to open one of the previously visited apps on the full screen.

Navigating the Screens
Android L & M

Lollipop and Marshmallow use a slightly different Navigation Bar, as shown below.

Navigation Bar: Android L & M

- The left-hand button above opens the previous screen.
- The button in the middle opens the central Home screen.
- The right-hand button opens a *revolving carousel* of "cards" representing the recently visited apps, also known as *Overview* or *Multitasking* mode, as shown below.

Overview mode

Recent Apps: Android L & M

Tap anywhere on the card for an app to open it on the screen. Tap the cross on an app to close the app.

Samsung Galaxy TouchWiz

Overview mode is also available on the Samsung Galaxy TouchWiz, after tapping the left-hand button, shown on page 21.

Shortcut Icons for Popular Android Apps

 All Apps: displays all the apps installed on a de-

 Google Chrome: a Web browser for navigating the Internet.

 Google Play Store: the source for downloading apps.

 Google: *search engine* used to find information on any subject.

 Google Earth: photos and satellite images of plac-es around the world, including Google Street View.

 Google Mail or **Gmail**: an electronic mail service.

 Email: electronic mail services of your choice.

 Play Music: install and play music, create

 Play Movies & TV: rent or buy then download.

 Google Maps: Searchable maps of the world with facilities to zoom in and zoom out.

Camera: Use either front facing camera for video calls and "selfies" or rear camera for general photog-

 Google Drive: cloud storage area which also includes free word processing and spreadsheet software.

 Dropbox: cloud storage area allowing photos and files, etc., to be accessed from any computer.

 Play Books: Download and read eBooks from the Google Play Store and create your own library.

 Kindle: Download and read eBooks from the Amazon Kindle Store.

 Skype: Internet telephone service allowing free video calls between computers around the world.

 Facebook: the popular social networking Web

 Twitter: social networking using "tweets" or short messages.

 Hangouts: send messages to your friends or start a video call.

 Google+: a social network allowing you to share updates and photos, etc.

Currents: displays news headlines and reports.

 Calculator: an easy to use basic calculator.

 Calendar: record future events, birthdays, etc., and receive notifications when imminent.

 Downloads: view documents, etc., that you've previously downloaded from the Internet.

 Photos: view, edit and manage your photographs.

 Clock: view the time in cities around the world and also use as an alarm clock and stopwatch.

 BBC iPlayer: watch live and catchup television.

 YouTube: watch free videos, e.g. amusing incidents, uploaded to the Internet for other people to share.

 Cloud Print: use the Web to print from anywhere to any printer.

The Google Play Store

Many of the apps listed on the previous pages are preinstalled on all Android new tablets and smartphones, while there are some that have been downloaded from the Play Store. Some manufacturers also preinstall apps of their own creation. The Google Play Store is the main source of Android apps, with over 2 milllion apps for a wide variety of activities.

To launch the **Play Store**, tap its icon (shown on the right) on the Home Screen or on the Apps screen. The **Google Play** window opens, showing the two main subject areas, **APPS & GAMES** and **ENTERTAINMENT**.

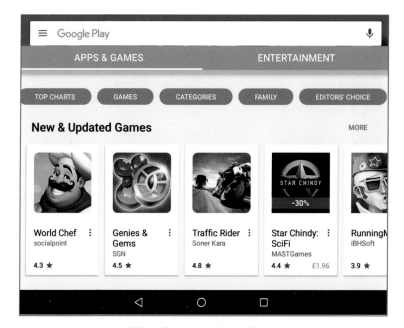

The Google Play Store

Although known as the Play Store, it actually contains apps in many categories other than games, such as business, music and utilities to help with the running of your device.

APPS & GAMES shown on the previous page includes apps on a wide range of subjects, as can be seen by tapping the **CATEGORIES** button.

CATEGORIES

All categories

Android Wear		Books & Reference	
Business		Comics	
Communication		Education	
Entertainment		Family	
Finance		Games	
Google Cast		Health & Fitness	
Libraries & Demo		Lifestyle	
Live Wallpaper		Media & Video	
Medical		Music & Audio	
News & Magazines		Personalisation	
Photography		Productivity	
Shopping		Social	
Sports		Tools	
Transport		Travel & Local	
Weather		Widgets	

Widgets

Categories of App in the Play Store

Browsing the Play Store for Apps

Select a **CATEGORY** such as **Health & Fitness**, shown below, then browse thorough to find an app you're interested in.

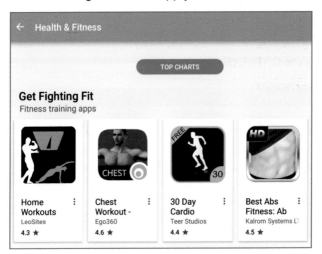

Health and Fitness Apps

Tap on the image of the app to read a description.

Many of the apps in the Play Store are free. If the app is not free a price is displayed at the bottom of the listing for the app, as shown below on the right. Tap on a free app to display the **INSTALL** button and tap this to download the app to your smartphone or tablet. If the app is not free, tap the price and then tap **BUY** shown below to complete the purchase online before tapping **INSTALL** .

Searching the Play Store for Apps

Tap the icon shown on the right to open the Play Store.

Typing Keywords

The search bar appears as shown below, ready for you to type the name of the app or widget you wish to search for.

Tap inside the blank search bar. The on-screen keyboard pops up automatically. Enter the keywords for the search, such as **flight simulator**, for example, and tap the search key (displaying a magnifying glass search icon) on the on-screen keyboard. A selection of apps matching your search keywords is displayed as shown below.

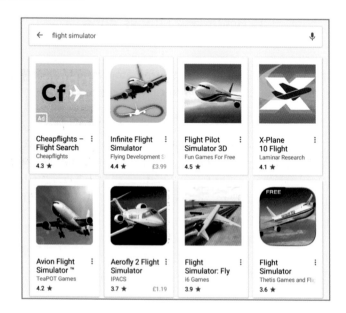

Using the Microphone: Speech Recognition

Tap the microphone icon shown on the right and below.

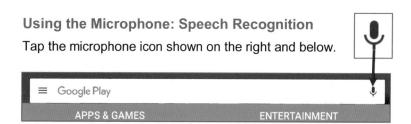

The small window shown below appears, requiring you to speak the keywords, such as **flight simulator**, for example,

Practise searching for a few apps using the microphone, such as **chess**, **route planner** and **sound recorder** for example.

Downloading and Installing an App

Tap the app you wish to install and if the app is not free, tap the price and buy the app online. Now tap **INSTALL** and wait a few minutes for the app to be downloaded to your Apps screen and your Home screen, shown below. Tap the icon to start using the newly installed app such as **Flight Pilot** in this example.

In-app Purchases

When you tap an app in the Play Store, you may see the words **In-app purchases** under the **INSTALL** button as shown on the right. This

means that although the app itself is free, you may be asked to make extra payments associated with the app. These payments might be for additional features or to purchase a "professional" version of the app rather than the basic or free edition. Some games allow you to buy additional features or even pay to advance to a higher level.

It's possible for someone else, especially children, to use your smartphone or tablet to run up a huge bill by making In-app purchases. The solution is to set a password which is required for all purchases from the Play Store.

Tap the Play Store menu icon shown on the left and below.

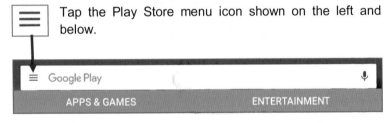

Then scroll down the menu and select **Settings**. From the settings menu tap **Parental controls** and then tap **Apps and Games**. Then type a suitable **PIN** number as shown below.

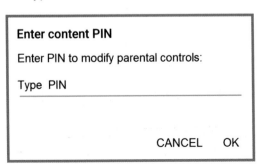

Customising the Favorites Tray

The Favorites Tray on the Home screens is shown below. The All Apps icon shown on the right and below is a fixture on the Favorites Tray — it cannot be moved or deleted. The other six icons can be moved and replaced with any other apps you prefer.

Removing an App from the Favorites Tray

Touch and hold the app you want to remove from the Favorites Tray until **X Remove** appears at the top of the screen. Drag the icon over **X Remove** and drop it, deleting the app. Removing an app from the Favorites Tray doesn't uninstall the app from the All Apps screen. Alternatively, move an app from the Favorites Tray and slide it onto another part of the Home Screen.

Moving an App to the Favorites Tray

Clear a space on the Favorites Tray by moving or removing an icon, as described above. To move an app on the Home screen to the Favorites Tray, tap and hold the icon, then drag the icon to the newly cleared space on the Favorites Tray. In the example below, the **ParkingMania** games app shown on the left of the Favorites Tray above has been removed and replaced by the shopping bag icon for the Play Store. The **Camera** app on the right of the Favorites Tray above has been replaced by a *folder* which includes the various **Google** apps.

As discussed shortly, folders can be created easily by dragging the icon for an app and dropping it over the icon for another app.

Customising Your Home Screen

When you start using a new tablet or smartphone, you can tailor the Home screen to suit your own requirements, as follows:

- Change the background colour or wallpaper.
- Copy apps from the Apps screen and place them on a personal page on the Home screen.
- Delete any apps and widgets you no longer need.

The Home screen actually consists of several separate panels or pages, some of which are initially blank. You can group apps into *folders*, which can be added to the Home screen and to the Favourites Tray. Folders are discussed on page 46.

Changing the Wallpaper on Your Home Screen

Hold your finger on an empty part of the Home screen until the wallpaper icon shown below appears.

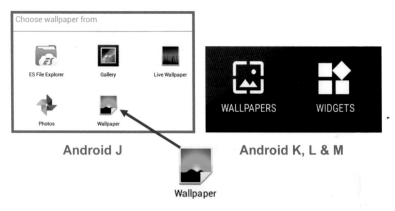

Android J   Android K, L & M

Wallpaper

Tap **Wallpaper** shown above and then tap your chosen pattern. Then tap **Set wallpaper**.

WIDGETS shown above are similar to apps but are used to display news and information, as discussed on pages 49-51.

Adding Apps to Your Home Screen

To make up a personal Home screen displaying only the apps you find most useful, open the Home screen where you want the apps to appear. Clear the screen of any apps and widgets you don't want. This is done by touching and holding the app or widget, then dragging onto **X Remove**, as described previously.

Tap the All Apps icon as shown on the right then touch and hold the app you want to copy to the Home screen. The Home screen opens. Keeping your finger on the app, slide it into the required position on the Home screen. Part of a personal Home screen is shown below.

A Personal Home Screen

Deleting Apps from the Home Screen

Tap and hold an unwanted app until **X Remove** appears at the top of the screen. Then drag the app over **X Remove** to delete it. Apps deleted from the Home screen are only *copies* — the apps still exist on the Apps screen.

Unlike apps removed from the Home screen, apps *uninstalled* from the Apps screen are completely removed from the tablet. If the uninstalled apps are needed in the future, they will need to be reinstalled from the *Play Store*.

Organising Apps in Folders

Folders containing several apps, as shown on the right, can be created on the Home Screen and on the Favorites Tray. For example, you could put the apps for **Facebook**, **Twitter**, **Skype** and **Google+**, shown below on the Home Screen, in a folder called **Social**.

Touch and drag the icons, one on top of the other, to form a single circular folder icon shown on the left below. Tap the folder icon to reveal the contents and to give a name to the folder. As shown below, tap **Unnamed Folder** and enter a name of your choice, **Social** in this example. Tap a folder icon to view and launch the individual apps within, as shown in the middle below.

Samsung Galaxy

On the Samson Galaxy hold down an icon for an app then drag it over **Create folder** which appears and name the folder.

Changing the Apps Background

This can be done after installing a new *launcher* app from the Play Store. Nova Launcher is a popular free app which allows you to make changes to the appearance of all the main versions of Android smartphones and tablets. Extra features are available if you buy the *Prime* version of Nova Launcher.

When you tap the central Home button on the Navigation bar as shown on page 32 and 33, you are given a choice of which launcher to use — the standard **Google Now Launcher** or **Nova Launcher**, as shown below. Select **Nova Launcher** and **JUST ONCE** to try the app initially.

Installing the app places a **Nova Settings** icon on the Apps screen, as shown on the right. Tap the **All apps** button shown on page 45 and then tap the **Nova Settings** button to open the menu shown in part below.

Select **App & widget drawers** as shown at the bottom of the previous page to open the window shown below.

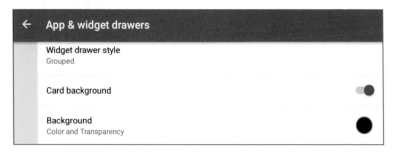

Tap the switch shown on the right above to set **Card background** to **On**. Then tap **Background** shown above to select from a choice of background colours. Now select the Apps screen to see the new background as shown in the examples below.

Android J & K   **Android L & M**

Changing the Background on the Apps Screen

Widgets

A *widget* is an icon used to display information such as a calendar, your most recent e-mails, the weather or a digital clock, as shown on the right. Widgets appear alongside of apps on the Home screen, as shown below.

Tapping a widget displays more information, such as the weather forecast, on the full screen.

Calendar widget

Digital clock widget

Widgets on the Home Screen

Viewing the Installed Widgets

Early versions of Android such as Jelly Bean have a Widgets tab on the Apps screen, as shown below. Tap this to see the Widgets already installed on your tablet or phone, on the Widgets Screen as shown below.

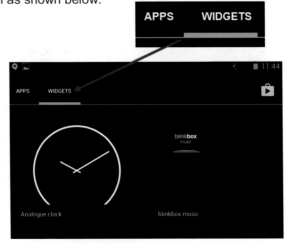

On later versions of Android such as KitKat, Lollipop and Marshmallow, tap and hold an empty part of the Home screen until the **WIDGETS** icon appears, as shown in the centre below.

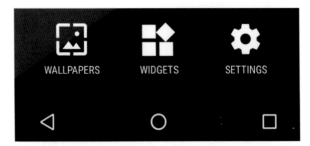

Tap the **WIDGETS** icon shown in the middle above to see the widgets already installed on your tablet or smartphone, such as the **Bookmarks** and **Calendar** widgets shown on the next page.

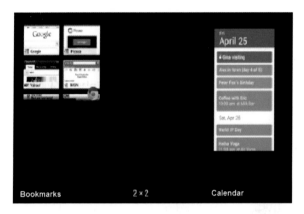

Widgets appear on the screen like Apps but usually display information which is regularly updated. Typical uses of widgets are:

- Local weather forecasts
- Your e-mail inbox
- An analogue or digital clock
- Newspaper headlines and articles
- A calendar
- Local traffic reports

Many widgets are already preinstalled on a new Android tablet or smartphone and more can be downloaded and installed from the Play Store, as shown at the bottom of page 38. You can create a special Home screen just for the widgets you find especially useful. To copy a widget from the Widgets screen to the Home screen, tap and hold the Widget. When the Home screen opens, slide the Widget into a suitable position.

Widgets can be copied, moved about and deleted, in a similar way to apps as described earlier in this chapter.

Key Points: Screens, Apps and Widgets

- The Android tablet or smartphone is "driven" by tapping icons representing apps and widgets.

- Apps are small applications or programs such as a web browser, a game or a drawing program.

- Widgets are small windows, usually displaying information such as a calendar, news or an e-mail inbox.

- The Apps screen shows all of the apps installed on the device.

- The Home screen consists of several panels which can be customized to display selected apps and widgets.

- Apps and widgets can be copied to the Home screen by touching and holding, then sliding onto the Home screen.

- Further apps and widgets can be downloaded from the Google Play Store. New apps are placed on the Apps screen and the Home screen automatically.

- At the bottom of every Home screen is a Favorites Tray which displays 6 icons for frequently used apps.

- The user can change 6 of the apps on the Favorites Tray.

- The All Apps icon is a fixture on the Favorites Tray.

- Widgets cannot be placed on the Favorites Tray.

- Related apps can be grouped together and placed in folders, such as Painting, Photography, Games, etc.

- Folder icons are circular, can have a name and can be placed on the Favorites Tray, also known as The Dock.

- Apps on the Home screen are only copies. Deleting them doesn't remove them from the Apps screen.

- The Navigation Bar at the bottom of all the screens has icons to open the Home screen, to display the last screen visited and show recently used apps.

More Android Features

Introduction

Previous chapters have looked at the setting up of an Android tablet or smartphone and the apps and widgets which are used to drive these small but extremely powerful and versatile devices. This chapter describes some more of the very useful features built into the Android operating system.

Google Now and Google Cards

These features enable Google to search for information using both voice and text queries. Google Cards automatically displays useful, real-time information for your current location and relevant to your interests.

Settings and Quick Settings

Used to switch important features on and off, make adjustments and tailor the Android to your own requirements.

Notifications

This screen keeps you up-to-date with new e-mail messages, calendar events, new downloads, Bluetooth, Wi-Fi, battery strength and aeroplane mode, as discussed shortly.

My Library

This is a widget that displays all the books, movies, music, etc., that are already on your Android tablet.

Calendar

Keeps track of all your appointments and sends reminders of imminent events, synchronised to your various devices.

Google Now

This is an extension to the popular Google search engine. Google Now employs *GPS* (Global Positioning System) satellite technology to pinpoint your current location. This is used to gather local information such as the weather and traffic conditions.

Google Now doesn't require any setting up — it's switched on by default. Google Now displays information as a series of cards on the screen. On Android Jelly Bean and KitKat, Google Cards are displayed by swiping up from the bottom of the Home Screen. On Android Lollipop and Marshmallow, swipe across to the right until the Google Now screen is displayed. (The cards and the Google Now settings are very similar for all versions of Android).

Menu button

Google Now Cards

Google Now Settings

Tap the menu button shown on the right and on the previous page. Then select **Settings** and **Now cards** to display the menu shown below. Here you can switch cards **ON** and **OFF** and select the topics to be notified about, such as weather, traffic and sports.

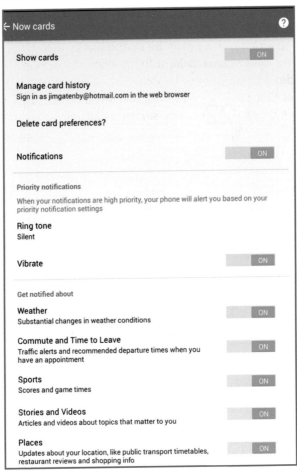

Google Now Card Settings

Searching in Google Now

Typing Keywords

Enter the keywords for a search, such as **weather in los cristianos**, by typing into the search bar at the top of the screen, using the on-screen keyboard.

Spoken Queries

You can also tap the microphone icon, as shown above and on the right. Then speak your query into the tablet. Using spoken queries is discussed in more detail on page 41. The voice search produces a spoken answer, as well as a Google Card, as shown above.

You will also see some traditional Google results, such as the one shown below, which you can tap to open Web pages relevant to your search.

Los Cristianos Weather - AccuWeather Forecast for Canary Islands ...
www.accuweather.com › World › Europe › Spain › Canary Islands
Get the **Los Cristianos weather** forecast. Access hourly, 10 day and 15 day forecasts along with up to the minute reports and videos for **Los Cristianos**, Spain ...

Perhaps you could experiment with a few spoken queries. For example, I spoke the question, "what is an android?". I received the spoken answer, "In science fiction a robot with a human appearance." This also appeared on a Google Card together with a list of traditional Google search results, as shown below.

Sporting Fixtures

If you enter or speak the name of a favourite sports team, such as Manchester City, Google Now produces a list of their latest results, news and fixtures, in both spoken and text form.

Travel Information

If you say or type "driving Ashbourne to London" for example, Google Now suggests routes and times and displays a map, as shown below. Similar information is available for flights and rail journeys.

Reminders in Google Now

Tap the Google Now menu button shown on the right and on page 54. From the menu you can tap to set **Reminders** of an event at a time or place.

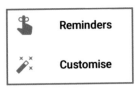

Tap the icon shown on the right to enter the details of the Reminder. Then enter the **Title**, **Time** and **Place**.

At the set time, an alarm rings and the Reminder is displayed on a card in Google Now. The Reminder also appears as a **Notification**, as discussed later in this chapter.

Reminder displayed as a Google Now card

Reminder displayed as a Notification

Notifications in Jelly Bean and KitKat appear against a black background. Otherwise they are essentially the same as the Notifications in Lollipop and Marshmallow as shown above.

Customising Google Now

You can tailor Google Now to display cards reflecting your interests. Select **Customise** from the menu shown at the top of the previous page.

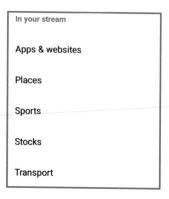

Tap **Apps & websites** shown above, then select **Yes** to receive Google Now cards based on your Web browsing activities and your location. In **Places** you can set your home and place of work, then receive traffic news about you journey. **Sports** allows you to enter the teams you wish follow. Select **Transport**, enter your normal method of getting around and Google Now will display relevant up-to-date information.

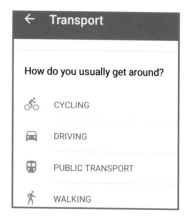

Settings for Google Now

Google Now requires the following settings:

> - Google Now **ON**
> - Location access **ON**
> - GPS satellites **ON**
> - Wi-Fi & mobile location **ON**

Switching Google Now On

If **Google Now** is not **ON**, when you swipe up from the bottom, or tap the **Google** icon on the Home Screen, you only see the basic Google screen, not the **Google Now** screen with cards, as shown on page 54. To turn **Google Now ON**, tap the menu icon shown on the right and on page 54 .

From the menu which appears, tap **Settings** and **Now cards** then tap to switch **Show cards ON**, as shown below and on page 55. This method is the same for all the main versions of Android although the **OFF/ON** switch is slightly different, as shown below.

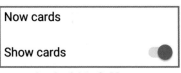

Android J & K   **Android L & M**

Location, GPS and Wi-Fi

Android Jelly Bean

Swipe down from the top right of the screen, to display the **Quick Settings** panel. Then select **SETTINGS** and under **PERSONAL** tap **Location access**. The three settings to enable Google Now to pinpoint your current location are shown below and should be **ON** or ticked. Tap anywhere in a row to change a setting.

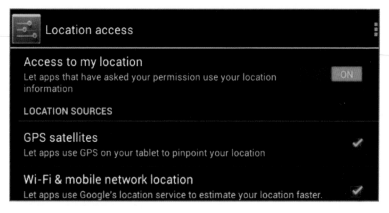

Android KitKat

After selecting **SETTINGS** as described above, tap **Location** and then tap **Mode** and make sure **High accuracy** is switched **ON** as shown below.

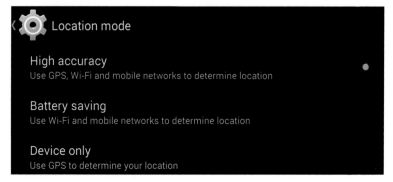

Android Lollipop and Marshmallow

Swipe down *twice* from the top of the screen to display the **Quick Settings** panel shown on page 64. If **Location** is already switched **ON,** you should see the **Location** icon in white, as shown on the right.

To check your **Location** settings, tap the **SETTINGS** icon on the **Quick Settings** panel and then tap **Location**, under **Personal**, as shown below.

Then make sure **Location** services are **ON**, by tapping the circular button on the right of the **Location** screen. Now tap **Mode** and select **High accuracy** as shown on the left below. This option makes sure that **GPS**, **Wi-Fi** and **mobile networks** are all used to identify your current location. The equivalent Samsung Galaxy TouchWiz screen is shown on the right below.

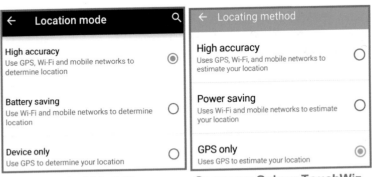

Your current location can now be used to find local facilities and weather and also to use your Android as a SatNav.

Quick Settings

Swipe down from the top of the screen, to display the **Quick Settings** window shown below.

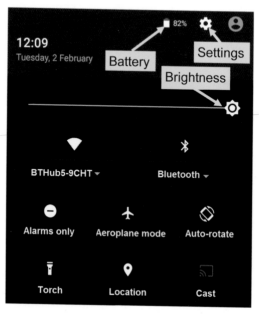

- **Settings** above opens the main **Settings** screen shown on page 68.

- **BTHub5-9CHT** shows that **Wi-Fi** is **ON**.

- **Auto-rotate** keeps the screen display upright when you turn the tablet through 90 degrees. Tap and select **ROTATION LOCKED** to fix the display to the tablet sides.

- **82%** shown above is the level of charge left in the battery.

- **AEROPLANE MODE** (or **FLIGHT MODE**) switches off the Internet so that the tablet can be safely used on a flight.

- **Bluetooth** is used to connect devices wirelessly over short distances, as discussed on page 152.
- **Torch** switches **ON** and **OFF** an LED for the rear camera.
- **Cast** mirrors the Android screen onto an HDMI TV, using the Google *Chromecast* dongle accessory if available.

Samsung Galaxy Quick Settings

Although the Samsung Galaxy TouchWiz has basically the same settings as standard Android, their colours, layout and design are different. Swipe down from the top of the screen to display the small group of settings shown below.

Then tap the **Settings** icon shown on the right and above. This opens the main settings screen, which lists groups of settings as shown in the small extract below. Tap on a heading in the list such as **Quick Settings** shown below. This opens the **Quick settings** panel shown on the next page.

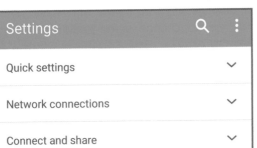

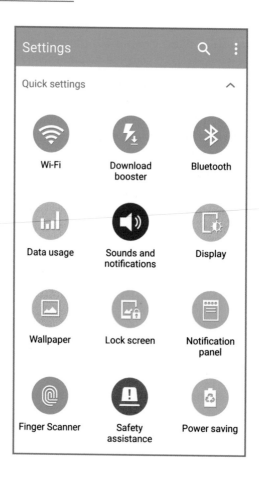

The **Quick Settings** windows shown above and on the previous page allows you to change some basic functions such as to switch **Wi-Fi ON** or **OFF**. The TouchWiz window has an icon to set the method of opening the **Lock screen** as shown above. These include setting a password or a PIN number, as discussed in Chapter 9.

For a more comprehensive list of settings you need to open the main **Settings** screen as discussed on the next few pages.

The Main Android Settings Screen

Opening the Settings Screen

The main **Settings** screen can be launched by opening the **Quick Settings** window, as discussed on the previous pages, and then tapping the appropriate **SETTINGS** icon, as shown below. The **Settings** icon is also shown at the top of the **Quick Settings** windows on pages 64 and 65.

Alternatively, tap the appropriate **All Apps** icon shown below then tap the **Settings** icon on the **Apps** screen.

 All Apps icons

Android   **TouchWiz**

 Settings icons

Jelly Bean   **Later Androids + TouchWiz**

As can be seen from the **Settings** screens on pages 68 and 69, the features listed are essentially the same on all the main versions of Android. There are only one or two differences such as the colour schemes and the layouts.

The **Settings** screens on pages 68 and 69 are referred to throughout this book.

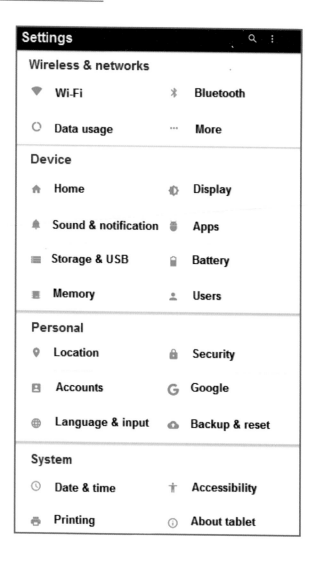

The **Settings** screen shown above is used on later versions of the standard Android O.S. such as Lollipop and Marshmallow. Earlier versions such as Jelly Bean and KitKat use the same main headings but with white text against a black background.

Samsung Galaxy TouchWiz Settings

As shown at the bottom of page 65, the TouchWiz settings screen can appear as a list of headings. Tap on the headings to expand each group of settings.

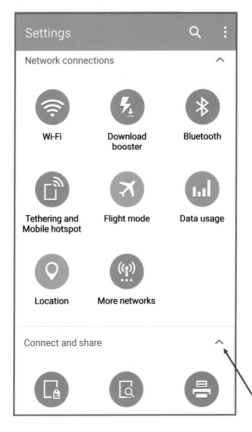

The above screenshot shows only a few of the settings for the Samsung Galaxy. Scroll vertically to see the other settings. To expand or collapse a group of settings, tap the small arrows shown on the right and above.

Notifications

At the top left of the of the Home and Apps screens you can see a group of small icons, similar to those shown below.

The icons above represent notifications or messages to let you know an event has occurred such as:

- An e-mail has been received.
- A file has been downloaded from the Internet.
- A screenshot has been captured.
- Some apps have ben updated.
- A calendar event is imminent.
- A system update is available.

To display your notifications swipe down from the top left of the screen. If a notification refers to an e-mail, tap twice to read the message. Once you've looked at a notification, it's removed from the list.

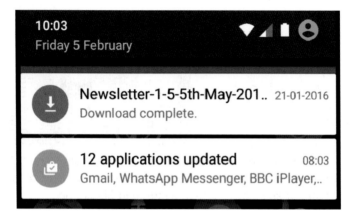

My Library

This is a widget that displays all the music, magazines, books, and movies that are installed on an Android smartphone or tablet. If necessary, clear a space on the Home screen by deleting unwanted apps and widgets as described on page 45.

Open the Widgets screens for your version of Android, as described on page 50. Swipe to scroll through the widgets until you see the **Play – My Library** widget as shown below left. Touch and hold this widget, then slide into a space on the Home screen. The **Play-My Library** window opens as shown below on the right.

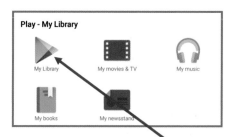

Tap the **MY LIBRARY** icon, shown on the right and in the window above right, to save thumbnails for all of your installed media — **My music**, **My books** and **My newsstand**, etc., on the Home screen as shown on the right. Tap a thumbnail in **My Library** to read a book, listen to music or watch a movie, for example.

If you tap individual icons such as **My music** or **My books**, shown above on the right, separate widgets for each medium are placed on the Home screen, rather than all of your media stored in **My Library**.

The Calendar

The Calendar includes the following features:

- Keeping a record of all your future events.
- Sending you notifications of imminent events.
- Synchronizing changes between various devices, such as your tablet, smartphone, laptop or desktop PC or Mac.

The Calendar is opened by tapping its icon, shown on the right, on the All Apps screen. The Calendar opens as shown on the bottom left below. A 3-bar menu button, shown here on the left, opens the menu shown on the right below. This has options to display **Days**, **Weeks** or **Months**. **Schedule** displays your events in a list which can be scrolled vertically. (On Jelly Bean the menu is opened by tapping the arrow shown on the right).

Calendar

Week

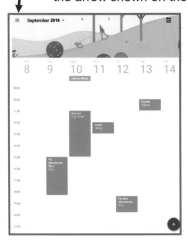

Scroll through the days, weeks or months by swiping horizontally.

Creating a New Event or Editing an Event

Tap the **New event** icon, shown on the right and at the bottom right of the calendar on the previous page. Then enter the details of the event such as the title, time and place.

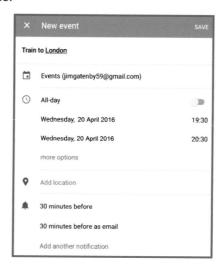

At the bottom of the **New event** screen you can set a reminder in the form of a notification or an e-mail. With a notification there is a beep and then an event, such as **Train to London** in this example, appears in the **Notifications** panel, as discussed on page 70. Tap the event name for further details.

To edit an existing event, double-tap the event's title on the Calendar, then tap the pencil icon which appears, as shown on the right. This opens the **Edit event** screen allowing you to amend the details.

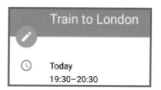

The Calendar Widget

A Calendar widget appears in the Widgets screen, as discussed on page 50 and 51. This can be copied to a suitable clear space on the Home screen. This is done by touching and holding the widget and then sliding it into position on the Home screen, as described in more detail on page 51. The Calendar widget lists all your forthcoming events, automatically updated with information from the Calendar app.

Calendar widget

Tap the Calendar widget to open the Calendar app full screen for editing existing entries or adding new events.

Syncing Your Calendar with All Your Computers

The Google Calendar can be created and viewed on all the common platforms — tablet, smartphone, laptop or desktop PC or Mac, etc. On a PC or Mac open **www.google.co.uk**. If necessary **Sign in** with your Gmail address (or **Sign up** for a new one). Then select the **Apps** icon on the top right of the screen, shown here on the right. From the drop-down window which appears, select the **Calendar** icon, shown below, to open the Calendar.

New events can be added to the Calendar on any of your devices. Any changes to the Calendar are automatically synced across to all the devices you are signed in to with your Gmail address and password.

5

Entertainment

Introduction

Amongst many other things, the Android smartphone or tablet is a versatile entertainment platform. The following activities are discussed in this chapter:

- eBooks — electronic books which may be downloaded from the Internet for reading *offline* at any time.

- Music, magazines, movies and games downloaded for free or bought or rented.

- YouTube — a Google-owned Web site enabling you to play free music and videos uploaded by other people.

- Live and catchup TV and radio.

The small size and light weight of an Android smartphone or tablet means you can use it literally anywhere — on a sofa, in bed or in a public place such as a restaurant. You can stow it in a bag and take it on holiday; most hotels now have free Wi-Fi so while you're away you can still go online for all your favourite Internet activities. The Android device may also be used for your personal in-flight entertainment, if the airline allows it. *Aeroplane mode* or *flight mode* should be switched on to prevent possible interference with the aircraft's instruments. This was mentioned on page 64 and only allows you to use the smartphone or tablet *offline*, i.e. not connected to the Internet. Such offline activities would include reading an e-Book which has been saved on the Internal Storage of the tablet, before boarding the aircraft.

eBooks

The Amazon Kindle, introduced in 2007, was a pioneer in the reading of electronic books or *eBooks*, especially on tablet computers. The Kindle uses its own heavily modified version of the Android operating system.

Millions of eBooks are available to be downloaded from the Amazon Kindle Store and saved on an Android device. Obviously the larger screen on the tablet gives it an advantage over the smartphone in this context. A device can keep more books on its Internal Storage than most people are ever likely to read.

- Android has its own app, *Play Books*, for reading eBooks and you can use it to download books from the Google Play Store, which contains millions of titles.

- You can also install the free Kindle App for Android tablets and obtain books from the Amazon Kindle Store.

You can always delete any eBooks you no longer want, in order to save space on the Internal Storage.

Google Play Books

When you first start to use an Android tablet or smartphone, there is already an icon for the Play Books app on the Apps screen. If you read a lot of eBooks, for easy access you may wish to copy the icon to the Favorites Tray as shown below, if it's not already there, as discussed on page 43.

Play Books

Tap the Play Books app shown on the right. On a brand new Android, you'll probably find a few books are already installed, as shown below in **My Library**.

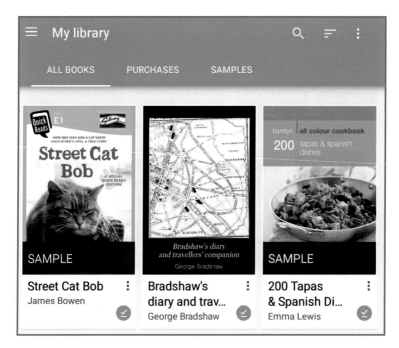

Tap the 3-bar menu icon shown on the right and next to **My Library** shown above.   This opens the menu shown on the right below, which includes the

Shop option. Tap **Shop** to open the Play Store Books as shown on the next page.

The Play Store can also be opened by tapping its shopping bag icon shown on the right below and on the Apps screen or   Home   Screen.   Then   select **ENTERTAINMENT** and **BOOKS**.

Browsing Through the Play Store Books

In the Play Store, as shown below, you can browse through the books under various headings such as **TOP SELLING** and **NEW RELEASES** shown across the top.

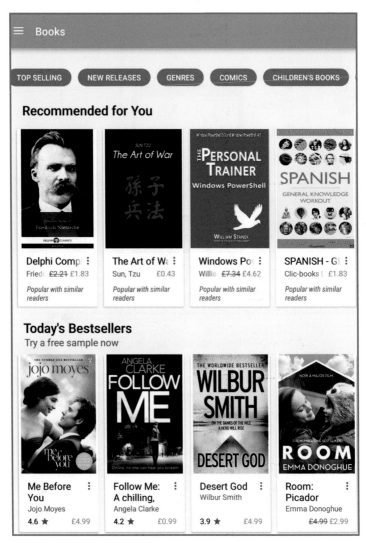

Tap **GENRES** shown near the top of the previous page to see the categories of books available, as shown in the extract below.

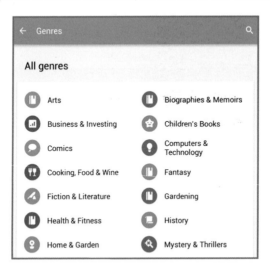

Select a genre, such as **Gardening** shown above, to see the range of those particular books available in the Play Store, as shown in the small sample below.

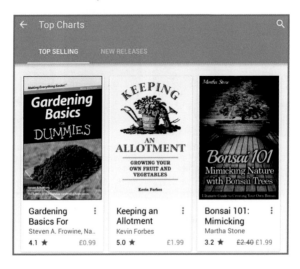

Searching for a Book in Play Books

Alternatively you can search for a particular book after tapping the search icon shown on the right. Type in the subject or the title of the book, replacing **Search for books** shown below.

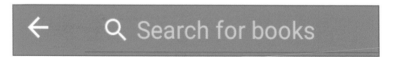

Or tap the microphone icon shown on the right below and speak the keywords.

For example, a search for **cats** produced numerous results, as shown in the small sample below.

Tap a book cover for more details, read a **FREE SAMPLE,** read reviews or to buy the book.

Alternatively tap the small three dot menu shown on the right and below, to buy the book, read a free sample, or add the book to a wish list. Buying a book requires a Google account with your bank account details.

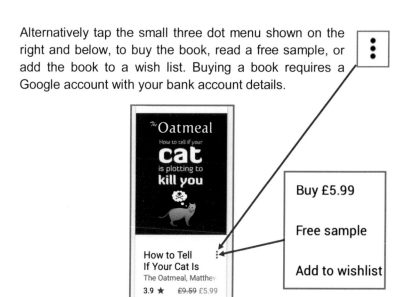

Buy £5.99

Free sample

Add to wishlist

Viewing the Books in Your Library

Tap the 3-bar menu shown on the right and select **My library** or **My books**. Books in your library which have also been downloaded and saved on your device display the tick icon shown below.

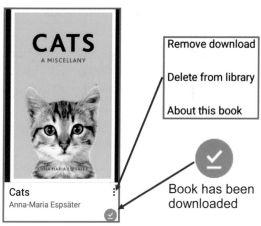

Remove download

Delete from library

About this book

Book has been downloaded

Reading Books Offline

Books in your library which display the tick shown on the previous page have been downloaded, i.e. copied to the Internal Storage of your tablet or smartphone. So they can be read when you're offline, i.e. not connected to the Internet. For example, you might want to download some books before going on holiday to a place where there is no connection to the Internet. Or on an aeroplane where you should select the **Flight Mode** or **Aeroplane Mode** (page 64) to avoid possible interference with the aircraft's own communications.

Deleting a Book from Your Device

When you've read a book you may wish to delete it from your Internal Storage to save space. Tap the 3-dot menu button shown on the right and on the previous page to display the menu shown below.

Remove download

Delete from library

About this book

Remove download above deletes the book from your Internal Storage, so it's no longer available to be read offline. However the book will still be available to read in your library, when you're connected to the Internet.

As shown above there is also an option to completely remove a book by tapping **Delete from library**.

About this book shown above gives a brief description of the book and details of the author, together with reviews by people who've read the book.

Downloading Books from Your Library

Some books in your library may not be available offline unless you've downloaded them. These can be seen after opening your library as discussed on page 81. Tap the 3-bar menu shown on the right and on page 81. To see which books have been downloaded and saved on your device, make sure the switch next to **Downloaded only** is **ON** as shown on the right below.

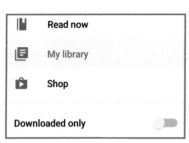

To see all of the books in your library make sure **Downloaded only** is switched **OFF** as shown above on the left.

Books in the library which are not available offline do not display the tick as shown at the bottom of page 81. To download these books, tap the 3-dot menu shown below and select **Download**.

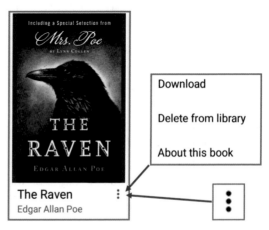

Reading an eBook

Tap the **Play Books** icon on the Apps screen, to open **My Library**. If necessary tap the 3-bar menu shown on   page 81 and select **My library**. Then tap the cover of the book you want to read. The book opens on the screen. Scroll backwards and forwards through the pages by swiping to

Play Books

the left or right, or tapping in the left and right margins. Tap anywhere on the text of the current page to view information about the page and to display various icons, etc., as shown in the top and bottom margins of the sample page below. Tap anywhere over the text again to switch off the icons and information.

Drag the blue ball slider shown below to advance rapidly forward or backward through the book.

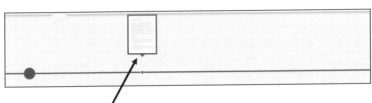

Tap the page thumbnail shown above to return to the page you were previously reading.

Across the top of the page, as shown above and on the previous page, the book title, author, chapter title and page number are displayed. The icons on the top right above have the following functions:

 Search for certain words and highlight them where they occur in the text.

 List chapter headings, page numbers and bookmarks.

 Change the brightness and formatting such as size of text, line spacing and font, etc.

 Open the menu shown on page 86, including options to add or remove a bookmark.

Bookmarks

Tap in the right-hand corner of the screen to add a bookmark in the top right-hand corner, as shown on the right. Tap a bookmark to remove it.

Using an Android Device as a Talking Book

The Play Books app has a **Read aloud** option. This feature can be used with many of the books and magazines in the Play Store. (As discussed on page 87, magazines can be obtained from the **NEWSSTAND** section of the Play Store).

To start reading aloud:

- Tap the cover of the book in My Library or Read Now.
- Tap anywhere on the text of a page to display the icons shown on page 85.
- Tap the 3-dot menu button also shown on page 85.
- From the menu which appears, tap **Read aloud**, as shown below on the right

The tablet or smartphone will now start reading the book aloud. To finish, tap over the text to display the 3-dot menu button and tap to display the menu shown on the right, but which now displays **Stop reading aloud**.

If you tap a book or magazine in **My Library** or **Read now**, which is not compatible with this feature, the menu displays, in greyed out text, **Read aloud unavailable**.

Tapping **Settings** shown on the right opens a menu which includes options to use the volume key (shown on page 16) to turn pages and to use a "**more natural voice**."

Original pages
About this book
Share
Add bookmark
Read aloud
Settings
Help & feedback

Original pages shown in the above menu displays a *scanned image* of the original book in the *PDF* (Portable Document Format) file format. Normally eBooks are saved in the *ePub* file format, also known as *flowing text*. The **Original pages** option is not available with some books.

Reading Magazines

Open the Play Store after tapping its icon, as shown on the right, on the Home screen or the Apps screen.

The Play Store has a **NEWSSTAND** feature, as shown below, where you can buy or subscribe to magazines in various categories. Some free magazines are also available.

Select **ENTERTAINMENT** as shown on page 37 then tap the **NEWSSTAND** button.

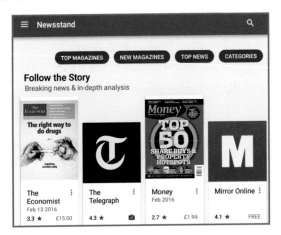

Magazines are installed in a similar way to books, as just described. To start reading a magazine in your library, tap **MY LIBRARY** on the Home screen, then tap **My newsstand** as shown below and discussed on page 71.

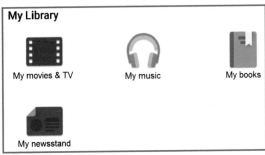

Music in the Play Store

Open the Play Store after tapping its icon on the Apps
screen, as shown on the right. Then tap **Entertainment**
and then **Music** as shown below.

In the **Music** section you can browse through various categories
such as **TOP SONGS**, **NEW RELEASES** and **GENRES**.

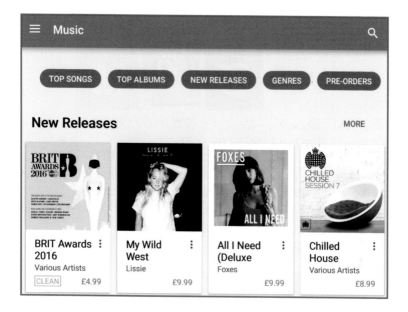

Alternatively tap the magnifying glass search icon,
shown on the right and above right, then enter the
name of a piece of music or an artist.

Tap the cover picture to buy a single or album. Or tap the
3-dot menu icon which, in this example, has the options
to **Buy £7.99** or **Add to wishlist** shown below.

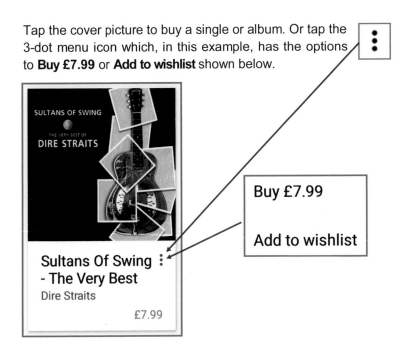

When you tap to buy a song or an album, in order to complete
the purchase you'll need to have an up-to-date Google account
with a valid banker's card. After completing the purchase the
music will be added to your library and downloaded and saved
on the Internal Storage of your smartphone or tablet.

Deleting Music

To save space on your Internal Storage you can delete a song by tapping the 3-dot menu button adjacent to the song's listing in your library, as shown on page 89. Then tap **Delete** shown below. Note also the other options such as adding to a playlist or sharing with someone else.

The Music App

Music can be played after tapping the Play Music icon shown on the right and located on the Apps screen.

The control bar along the bottom of the music screen, shown below, has the usual Play, Forward, Back and Pause buttons. You can also give a piece of music either a "thumbs up" or a "thumbs down" as shown on the right below.

The volume control ,key is located on the side of a smartphone or tablet as shown on page 16.

Movies and TV

Open the Play Store as discussed previously and select **ENTERTAINMENT** and then **MOVIES & TV** as shown below.

You can then browse through the various categories such as **TV**, **GENRES** and **FAMILY** shown below.

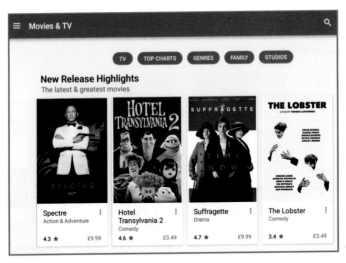

Tap a cover picture as shown above. This will allow you to buy or rent the movie or TV, etc.

Tap the icon shown on the right to add the movie or TV to your **wishlist** for possible purchase later.

Rental Period

You can see how long you can rent a movie, etc., after tapping the movie cover picture and then tapping **READ MORE** on the information page. For example, "start watching within 30 days of renting it and finish within 48 hours of starting to watch it."

Watching Movies and TV

Tap the icon shown on the right on the Apps screen or in **My Library** shown on page 87. Then tap the movie cover picture or tap the play button.

My movies & TV

Downloading a Movie for Viewing Offline

To make a movie watchable offline, tap the **Download** icon on the movie graphic, shown on the left below. The circle starts to fill with red "ink" and when completely full the download is complete. The icon then displays a white tick in a red circle, as shown below.

A *notification*, as shown below, should also be displayed when you swipe down from the top of the screen.

Streaming versus Downloading

Media such as music, movies, eBooks, etc., are held as *files* on the Internet server computers of companies such as Google, Amazon, YouTube, Spotify and Netflix. Movie and video files are very large and take a relatively long time to transfer over the Internet. Now, with high speed fibre optic broadband Internet, it's more feasible to make a copy of videos, etc., on your Android smartphone or tablet.

However, movie, video and music files that you buy or rent from a service such as the Play Store are not automatically saved on the Internal Storage of a smartphone or tablet. They remain in the clouds on the Internet and you must be online to enjoy them.

Streaming

A streamed media file is *temporarily* transmitted to your Android smartphone or tablet over the Internet and you access it in *real time*. A copy is *not saved* on the tablet. A *buffer* may be used to temporarily store "chunks" of the video, etc., to guard against interruptions in the streaming process. You will need to be connected to the Internet to access a file again in the future.

Streaming Services

Apart from the Google Play Store, some of the leading services for streaming music, movies and TV episodes include Netflix, Spotify, Amazon and YouTube. Apps are available for these services in the Play Store, if they are not already installed on your smartphone or tablet.

Downloading

A *copy* of a media file is transferred over the Internet and **saved** on the Internal Storage of the tablet. You can access this eBook, movie, etc., at any time in the future, without being connected to the Internet. Downloaded files such as books and movies can be used in *Aeroplane mode* and places where there is no Wi-Fi.

YouTube

YouTube is a Web site, owned by Google, which provides a platform for people to share videos which they've recorded themselves. These can rapidly become very popular and "go viral", watched by millions of people around the world.

To launch YouTube, tap the icon shown on the right, on the Apps screen. The YouTube screen shows a long list of video clips which can be scrolled up and down by swiping through various categories.

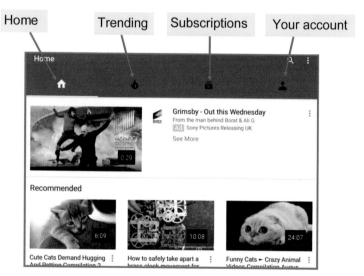

To put a video of your own on YouTube tap the **Upload** icon shown on the right. This appears at the bottom right of the YouTube screen. Then browse your smartphone or tablet and select the video. After adding a title and a description, in **Add Details**, set the **Privacy** level at **Public**, **Unlisted** or **Private**. Finally tap **UPLOAD** shown on the right to post your video on YouTube for all to see (depending on your privacy setting).

Live and Catchup Television and Radio

The Google Play Store includes the free BBC iPlayer app. This can be installed on your tablet as described in Chapter 3. Tap the icon shown on the right to open the BBC iPlayer as shown below.

You can scroll the red bar at the top to select different channels or select to watch today's live television or select a previous day to catch up with programmes from the last week. Tap **Menu** shown above left to choose from programmes in various **Categories** such as **Comedy**, on different channels including radio.

Watching TV

Tap anywhere on the picture for the episode, programme, etc., and then tap the play button. The screen display has the normal play, pause and volume control buttons.

Games

There are thousands of games in the Google Play Store, many of them free, though some include *In-app purchases* to buy extras, as discussed on page 42.

Games are downloaded and installed as discussed in Chapter 3 and so they will be available to play offline. Games can be removed from your smartphone or tablet as discussed on page 45.

If you play a lot of games, you may wish to organize them into *folders*, as discussed on page 46. In this example, the four games on the right have been grouped into a single folder as shown below.

Candy Crush :
Saga
King
4.3 ★

ParkingMania   Solitaire

Robbery Bob   Chess Free
My Games

Games folder

Browsing the Web

Introduction

The Android smartphone or tablet gives us access to millions of Web pages, containing the latest information on any subject you can think of.

The Chrome Web browser is a Google product, like the Android operating system itself. Chrome enables you to search millions of Web pages quickly and easily and displays the results in an attractive and readable format. The Google search engine is the world's leading Web search program on all platforms – smartphone, tablet, laptop and desktop computers. So it's not surprising that an Android device is an ideal tool for browsing the Internet to find information. This activity alone justifies the purchase of an Android smartphone or tablet, not to mention its many other functions such as news, social networking and entertainment, discussed later in this book.

Some of the main functions of Google Chrome are:

- To search for and display information after entering or speaking *keywords* into the Google search engine.

- To access Web pages after entering an *address*, such as **www.babanibooks.com**, into the browser.

- To move between Web pages by tapping *links* or *hyperlinks* on a Web page and move forwards and backwards between Web pages.

- To *bookmark* Web pages for revisiting at a later time.

Launching Google Chrome

To launch Google Chrome, tap its icon on the Apps screen or on the Favorites Tray, shown below.

The search bar across the top of the screen, shown below, is the place to start your Web browsing activities. Here you enter either the address of a Web site or *keywords* which should pinpoint the subject you are interested in.

Entering the Address of a Web Site

Every Web site has a unique address, known as its *URL*, or *Uniform Resource Locator*. A typical Web address is :

www.babanibooks.com

Type the URL into the search bar, as shown below and tap the **Go** key or the arrow key (shown on the right) on the on-screen keyboard.

For a complicated address you may need to enter the URL in full, as shown above. However, in practice you'll often find you don't need to be too pedantic; simply entering **babanibooks**, for example, will lead you to the required Web site.

Using the Microphone

Instead of typing the URL, as discussed above, you might prefer to tap the microphone icon shown on the right and on the previous page. Then speak the Web address.

After entering the address of the Web site into the search bar and pressing **Go** or the arrow key on the on-screen keyboard, the Web site's Home Page should quickly open on the screen, as shown in the extract below.

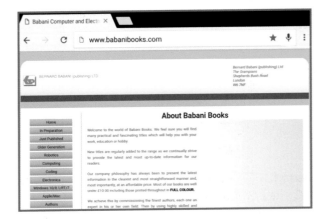

The Keyword Search

This is used to find out about a particular subject rather than visiting a Web site whose address you already know, as discussed on the previous page. For example, suppose you want to find out about the Great Wall of China. Enter the keywords as shown on the next page or tap the microphone icon and speak them.

As you start entering the keywords, Google starts making suggestions underneath, as shown on the next page. If correct, this *predictive text* will save you typing all of the keywords which make up the search criteria.

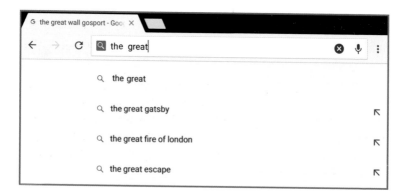

After completing the entry of the keywords and tapping the **Go** or arrow key on the on-screen keyboard, a list of Google search results is displayed, as shown in the small sample below.

As shown on the previous page, there's no need to use capital letters when typing the search criteria — **the great wall of china** yields the same results as **The Great Wall Of China**.

Only a few sample results are shown at the bottom of the previous page but a search often yields millions of results. Google places the most significant results near the top of the list. However, some results may be irrelevant to a particular search. For example, anyone studying the Great Wall of China may not be particularly interested in the **All you can eat buffet — Review of Great Wall Chinese Restaurant** which appears in the results of the search.

The blue heading on a search result, shown below, represents a *link* to a Web page which contains the keywords you've entered.

Great Wall of China: Great Wall Tours, Facts, History, Photos
www.travelchinaguide.com › china_great...

Tap a link to have a look at the Web site as shown below.

Great Wall of China - Wikipedia, the free encyclopedia
en.wikipedia.org

As shown on the previous page, you can also see the results of your search organised in various categories such as **IMAGES**, **MAPS**, **VIDEOS** and **NEWS**, etc.

Surfing the Net

On the Web page below, words highlighted in blue by the Web page designer are *hyperlinks*, also known simply as *links*.

Tap the blue text link shown above to open further relevant Web pages. Each new page will probably have further links to open a succession of Web pages.

As discussed shortly, Google Chrome keeps a log of the Web pages you've visited in the **History** feature. Also, any pages which you think you may wish to revisit in the future can be saved as **Bookmarks**, as discussed later in this chapter.

Searching for Anything

The Web is surely the world's largest and most up-to-date encyclopaedia covering almost every known subject, no matter how bizarre. For example, type any task, such as riding a horse and numerous Web sites offer helpful advice, often including step -by-step videos.

horsebreedsinfo.com
Images may be subject to copyright

Try typing a few diverse keywords into Google Chrome and see how easy it is to find good information on virtually any subject.

mending a puncture	sopwith camel	st paul de vence
capability brown	ann of cleves	growing orchids
ssd	tintagel	halebop
robert stevenson	ftse index	tim peake

Previously Visited Pages

As you move between Web pages, you may wish to briefly revisit a page. The back and forward buttons shown on the right and below allow you to quickly move between recently visited pages. Tapping the circular arrow button on the right and below reloads the latest version of a Web page. (For speed, the Chrome browser may load an earlier version of a Web page).

As you move forward or back between Web pages, the keywords from each search, such as **shearing a sheep**, are displayed on the tab at the top of the screen, replacing the keywords **mending a puncture** of the previous search, as shown below.

Tabbed Browsing

When you do a search in Google Chrome and then proceed to surf the Web, as described earlier, there may be only one tab displaying only the current Web page, as described at the bottom of the previous page. However, Chrome allows you to open each Web page in a tab of its own, so that all the tabs are visible along the top of the screen, as shown in the example below.

This makes it easy to move straight to a particular Web page, rather than moving through them all one at a time using the backwards and forwards buttons. Tap a tab to open that Web page. With a large number of Web pages open, the tabs may be stacked on top of each other and can be moved around by sliding or gently swiping left or right.

Opening a Web Page in Its Own New Tab

Tap the **New tab** icon shown on the right and below.

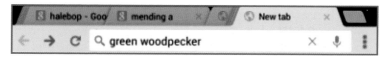

A **New tab** appears, as shown above on the right, with the search bar ready for you to enter your search criteria by typing or speaking. After carrying out the search and selecting a Web page from the list of results, this page appears on its own tab. The search criteria, in this case **green woodpecker**, appear on the top of the tab, as shown below.

Using the Google App

In the previous examples, Google Chrome was opened by tapping its icon on the Favorites Tray or on the Apps or Home screens. You can also start to launch Chrome after tapping the Google icon shown on the right, on the Apps screen. Then enter the search criteria, such as **red kite** in this example, in the Google search bar, as shown below.

Google

The search results open in Google Chrome, in a new tab, **red kite**, in this example, as shown below. Tap on a link in the search results to open a Web page you want to look at.

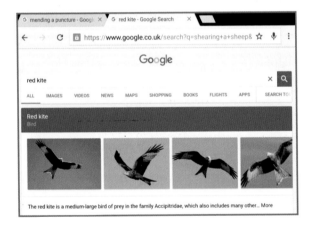

To switch to another Web page from a previous search, simply tap its tab, such as **mending a puncture**, shown above.

Closing a Tab

Close a tab by tapping the **X**, as shown on the right.

Bookmarking a Web Page

A series of *bookmarks* can be created to enable you to quickly return to your favourite Web pages at any time. With the required Web page open on the screen, tap the star-shaped bookmark icon as shown on the right and on the right of the search bar below.

The bookmark icon changes to blue and a note at the bottom of the screen informs you that the page has been bookmarked. Tap the blue Edit link to replace the default name for the bookmark. Tap the 3-bar menu button shown on the right and above and from the menu, (shown on page 108), select **Bookmarks** to open the screen shown below.

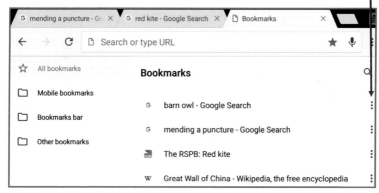

Tap the name of bookmark, such as **barn owl** in the list above, to revisit that Web page and open it on the screen.

Tap the 3-dot menu to the right of a bookmark above to open the menu shown on the right, including options to **Edit** and **Delete** the bookmark.

Displaying Your Browsing History

Google Chrome keeps a record, in chronological order, of all the Web pages you've visited. Tap the main 3-dot menu button at the top right of the Chrome screen, shown on the upper right. Then select **History** from the menu shown on the right. This lists all of the Web pages you've visited in chronological order, with the latest at the top. To revisit a Web page, tap its name in the **History** list shown below.

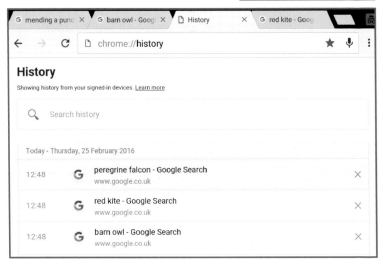

Clearing Your History

Tap the **X** on the right of a Web page, as shown above, to delete it from **History**. Tap **CLEAR BROWSING DATA...** at the bottom of the screen to open a menu to delete your **Browsing history**, amongst other things.

Communication and Social Networking

Introduction

This chapter describes the various ways an Android smartphone or tablet can be used to communicate with other people. Some of the main apps used for these activities are:

Gmail

Google e-mail used by businesses, friends and families to send messages, documents and photos all over the world.

Skype

Free worldwide *voice* and *video* calls between computers.

Facebook

The most popular *social networking* website. Enter your personal *profile* and *timeline* and make *online friends* with people having similar backgrounds and interests.

Twitter

Another very popular social networking site, based on short text messages (*140 characters maximum*) which can be read by anyone who chooses to follow the originator.

WhatsApp

This is an extremely popular free service for sending text messages, photos and documents using smartphones.

Instagram

This is a social networking site which makes it easy to take photos and videos and share them with other people.

Electronic Mail

An e-mail message includes text similar to a letter and can also include photos and documents, known as *attachments*. *Replies* can easily be sent to the originator and to all other recipients and a message can also be *forwarded* to someone else.

You can maintain an *address book* for all your contacts and *import* into it files of contacts from other e-mail services.

Gmail is a web-based e-mail service, so you can access your electronic correspondence from anywhere in the world. All you need is a connection to the Internet and your Gmail username and password, as discussed on page 26.

The Gmail icon shown above gives access to Gmail and any *other e-mail services you use*. After tapping the Gmail icon, tap the 3-bar menu button and select the account to use, as shown on the right.

Creating a Message

Tap the **Compose** icon at the bottom right of the screen, shown here on the right. The **Compose** screen opens, as shown on the next page. Enter the main recipient's e-mail address in the **To** bar. Tapping the small arrow on the far right of **To** opens two new lines for recipients who will receive either Carbon copies (**Cc)** or Blind carbon copies (**Bcc**). The latter don't know who else has received a copy of the message. Then enter the **Subject** followed by the main text. Tap the paperclip icon to browse for and attach any files you wish to include, before tapping the send button shown on the next page.

Attach file — Send

From   jimgatenby@hotmail.com

To   stellaaustin86@gmail.com

Barn owls

Hi Jill

These are the barn owls in the nest near our house, last year.

I have also attached a pdf copy of your boarding pass for tomorrow's flight.

Attached photo

Attached pdf file

Receiving an E-mail

The recipient can read the e-mail in their *Inbox*. They will see the sender's name and the text and photos as shown above.

To open an attached document, tap its name or the paperclip icon, as shown on the right. Tap the star icon on the right to mark the e-mail as a *favourite*. Icons at the bottom of the message, as shown below, allow you to reply to the sender, reply to all recipients of the message or forward the e-mail to someone else.

Reply   Reply all   Forward

Skype

This app allows you to make *voice* and *video* calls all over the world. Calls over the Internet are free. If you use a smartphone or tablet to dial a phone number there is a charge, for which you need credit in a Skype account. You can also send photographs and instant text messages or make and send a video.

The Skype app in the Google Play Store is free and, if necessary, can be installed as described in Chapter 3.

Start Skype by tapping its icon on the All Apps screen, as shown on the right. Then sign in using an existing Skype username and password or a Microsoft account, or create a new Skype account. When you sign in, contacts from your address book are displayed, as shown below.

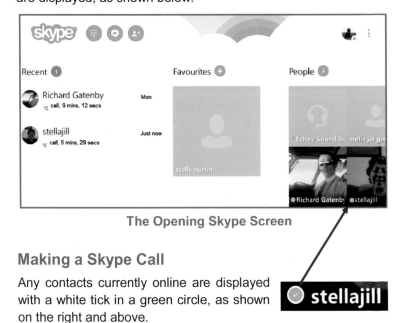

The Opening Skype Screen

Making a Skype Call

Any contacts currently online are displayed with a white tick in a green circle, as shown on the right and above.

Tap the name or thumbnail of a contact who is currently online.

The following icons are available when making a Skype call:

Start a voice only call   Start a video call

When you call a contact, their photo and name appear on your screen. The functions of the icons are listed below.

Making a Skype call

Receiving a call

Receiving a Skype Call

When someone "Skypes" you, the smartphone or tablet will emit a distinctive ring and the caller's name appears on the screen as shown above on the right. Tap the green phone icon shown on the right above to answer the call.

The Main Skype Icons

   Answer a video or voice call

   Switch video on or off

   Switch microphone on or off

  Show dialling pad and messages

  End or reject a call

Facebook

Facebook is the biggest social network, with over a billion users all over the world. To join Facebook, you must be aged over 13 years and have a valid e-mail address. You can access Facebook using the Android Facebook app, if necessary installed from the Play Store, as discussed in Chapter 3. You also need to *sign up* for a Facebook account and in future *sign in* with your e-mail address and password.

Facebook

First you create your own *Profile* in the form of a *Timeline*, as shown below.

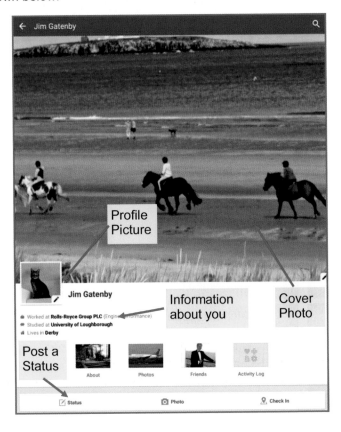

This can include personal details such as your schools, employers and hobbies and interests. Facebook then provides lists of people with similar interests, who you may want to invite to be Facebook *friends*. Anyone who accepts will be able to exchange news, information, photos and videos with you.

A Profile Picture or Cover Photo can be changed after tapping anywhere within the image.

Security and Privacy

The *audience selector* shown on the right appears against the items of personal information in your profile. Tapping the audience selector displays a drop-down menu, as shown below, enabling you to set the level of privacy for each item, ranging from **Public** to **Only me**. **Public** means *everyone* can see the information, including people you don't know.

Obviously privacy is a major issue with social networks and great care should be taken with regard to safety and security. Without careful attention to your privacy settings as shown above, your information may be accessible to a worldwide audience.

Status Updates

These are used to post your latest information and news and usually consist of a short text message and perhaps one or more photos. Tap **Status** on the bottom left of the Facebook screen, shown on page 114, to open the **Post to Facebook** window shown below. Tap **To:** to select the audience — **Public**, **Friends**, **Only Me**, etc. Then enter the text of your post, replacing **What's on your mind?** shown below.

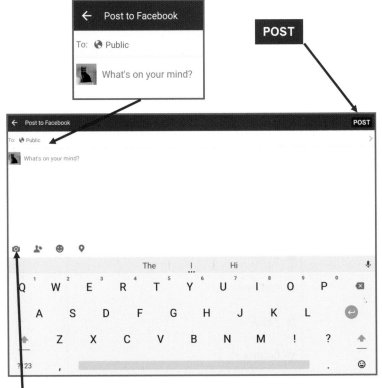

Tap the camera icon shown on the left and above to insert a photo after browsing the Internal Storage of the smartphone or tablet. Finally tap **POST**, shown on the right above, to deliver your status update.

Twitter

Like Facebook, Twitter is a social networking website used by hundreds of millions of people. There is a free app for Twitter in the Google Play Store. If necessary, the app can be installed as discussed in Chapter 3. 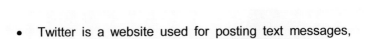 Signing up to Twitter is free. Once signed up you can either use your e-mail address and password to sign in or you can enter your Twitter username such as **@jimsmith**. Some of the main features of Twitter are:

- Twitter is a website used for posting text messages, known as *tweets*, of up to 140 characters in length.
- You can include a 160 character *personal profile* on your Twitter page.
- Photographs can be posted with a tweet.
- Twitter is based on people *following*, i.e. reading the tweets of other people, such as celebrities, politicians and companies marketing their products or services.
- You can follow anyone you like, but you can't choose who follows you. If you have no followers, anything you post on Twitter will remain unread. You could encourage your friends and family to follow you and each other on Twitter, to share your latest news.
- *Hashtags*, such as *#climatechange*, for example, make it simple for other people to find all the tweets on a particular subject. The hashtag is included within a tweet. Tapping the hashtag displays all the tweets on that subject, which might be a campaign or a debate.
- If you like a tweet, it can be *retweeted* to all of your followers, together with comments of your own.
- You can send *replies* to a tweet.

Sending a Tweet

Tap the quill ion at the bottom left of the Twitter Home screen then start typing your message, as shown below.

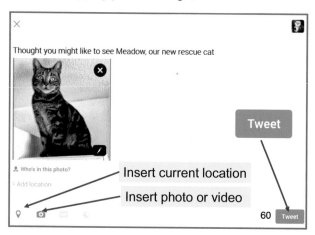

Insert current location

Insert photo or video

The number **60** on the bottom right above is the number of letters still available to be used, out of the maximum of 140 allowed.

Tapping the left-hand icon above uses the GPS system in your tablet or smartphone to pin-point your current location and include this as a note in the Tweet.

Inserting a Photo into a Tweet

Tapping the camera icon shown above and on the right displays the three icons shown below.

The left-hand icon above allows you to take a photo with your device's in-built camera and then insert the photo into the Tweet. Videos can be created and inserted using the centre icon. The icon on the extreme right allows you to browse the Internal Storage on your device to find a photo or video to insert.

When the tweet is finished, tap the blue **TWEET** button, shown near the top of the previous page. Your followers will see your tweet on their Twitter Home screen, as shown below.

To display the tweet and image in full and to show further options, tap anywhere on the text of the tweet.

Displaying or Hiding Images in a Tweet

The timeline is a list of tweets from the people you follow and also includes your own tweets. If a tweet includes a photo there is an option to display the image within the tweet, as shown at the top of the previous page. However, with too many images filling up your screen it may be difficult to read your timeline. So you may wish to hide the images from the list of tweets.

Tap the 3-dot menu button at the top of the timeline as shown on the right and at the top of the previous page.

From the menu which appears tap **Settings** then **Data**. The check box shown below on the right can be either ticked, as shown, to display the images or blank to hide the images.

Switch off the image previews by unticking the check box shown above. Instead of images, a blue text links appears in the tweet in the timeline, **pic.twitter.com/1QO4oZ9hDR** shown below.

James Gatenby @jimgatenby
Thought you might like to see Meadow, our new rescue cat pic.twitter.com/
1QO4oZ9hDR

Tap the blue text link shown above to display the image in full.

Responding to a Tweet

When you display a tweet in full, as discussed on page 119, the following toolbar appears at the bottom of the screen. (You may need to scroll upwards to see toolbar).

Tapping the above icons enable you to respond to a tweet in various ways. Reading from left to right, they are:

 Send a **Reply**.

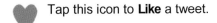 **Retweet** a tweet you have received from someone you are following. This forwards the tweet to your followers.

Tap this icon to **Like** a tweet.

Send a *link* to other people to **Share** a tweet using various apps and features as shown in the sample below.

 Tap this icon, shown at the top right of this page, to delete a tweet from your timeline.

WhatsApp

This is a messaging service which has become extremely popular in the last few years, with over a billion users worldwide. It's full of useful features while still being very easy to use.

WhatsApp is compatible with all of the popular smartphones such as Androids, iPhones and Blackberries. So you can communicate with friends having different makes of smartphone. Your WhatsApp contacts must be on your phone contacts list and have WhatsApp Messenger installed from their app store.

WhatsApp Messenger is a free app which can be installed from the Play Store, as shown below. Downloading and installing apps is discussed in Chapter 3.

As shown above, WhatsApp is designed for phones. If you try to install WhatsApp on a Wi-Fi only tablet the following message appears in the Play Store.

There are third party apps to enable WhatsApp to be used on tablets and a Web version is available for use with laptops and desktop computers.

WhatsApp allows you to communicate with friends anywhere in the world and there are no subscription fees. You can use a Wi-Fi connection via a router in your home or use a wireless hotspot in a public place such as a café or airport, as discussed in Chapter 10. This will allow you to make free worldwide phone calls in a similar way to Skype, discussed earlier in this chapter. Or you can connect using the 3G/4G Internet connection on your phone.

Some of the main features of WhatsApp are:

- Free worldwide telephone calls using your Internet connection.
- Sending and receiving photos, videos, voice messages and files
- Group chats with friends, family, colleagues, etc.
- Share your current *location* in a message.
- WhatsApp uses your phone number rather than a username, password or PIN, etc

After you install WhatsApp, and tap **OPEN**, you need to agree to let WhatsApp access your files and contacts. Then enter your smartphone number. WhatsApp sends a message to verify your phone number. Next add your name and an optional photo.

Launching WhatsApp

Open WhatsApp by tapping its icon on the Home Screen or Apps screen, as shown below.

As shown below, there are three main sections in WhatsApp, **CALLS**, **CHATS** and **CONTACTS**. As discussed earlier, WhatsApp searches your phone contacts and identifies anyone who is already a user of WhatsApp. Then they are added to your WhatsApp **CONTACTS** list as shown below. If you want to communicate with anyone else via WhatsApp you need them to download and install the app. **CALLS** logs the phone calls you've made. **CHATS** lists your conversations in a scrollable series of text, pictures and voice messages as shown on page 126.

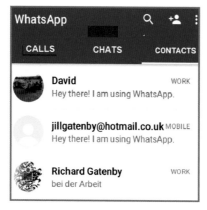

Creating a WhatsApp Message

When you tap on a contact's name for the first time, a blank screen appears allowing you to enter a message.

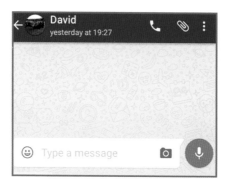

There are numerous additional features of WhatsApp to enhance a message, apart from the basic text entry bar shown at the bottom of the previous page. These are launched by the icons shown below and at the bottom of page 124.

 Make an ordinary phone call.

 Insert a document, file, photo or video, etc., or insert your current location, as shown below.

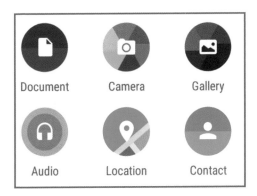

 Add an e*moticon* facial image to express the mood of a message.

 Take a photo using your phone's forward facing camera or take a *selfie* using the backward facing camera.

 Switch between front and rear facing cameras (This appears after the camera icon shown above is selected.)

 Tap and hold to make a voice recording to send with the message.

125

After you type your message, tap the **Send** button shown on the right and below.

Receiving a WhatsApp Message

When you send a WhatsApp message to one of your contacts, they will see a notification if they are online. If they are offline, the message will be available next time they launch WhatsApp.

As shown below, your exchange of messages with a contact becomes a running conversation, which can be scrolled vertically. To view a conversation, select **CHATS** as shown on page 124 and then tap the name of the contact.

Attach a photo, video, or file, etc.

Play voice message

Enter your reply

Send message

Your contact can enter a reply and tap the **SEND** button shown above. **14.32** above shows the time the message was sent. The tick on the left shows the message has been sent while the tick on the right indicates that the message has been read.

Deleting a Message

Tap and hold then tap the dustbin icon that appears.

Instagram

This is an extremely popular app for taking, editing and sharing photos and videos. Instagram is owned by Facebook and shares many of the features of the world's leading social networking sites such as Facebook and Twitter. These include creating your own user Profile, in which you display your photos and videos.

Like the other social networks, you can follow people who interest you and you can allow other people to follow you.

Instagram is a free app in the Play Store and can be installed on Android smartphones and tablets as discussed in Chapter 3. An icon is placed on the Apps screen, as shown on the right.

After opening Instagram, you are asked to sign in with either a Facebook account or an e-mail address and password. A list of suggestions of people for you to follow is displayed, as shown below. You may also be asked if you want to follow friends who are on both Facebook and Instagram.

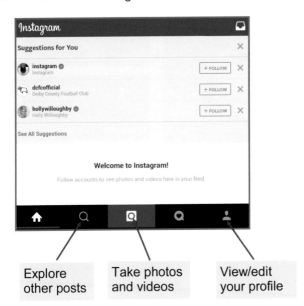

Tap the camera icon shown on right and on the previous page to take either a photo or a video, using the menu bar as shown below.

Tap the blue circle to take a photo or tap and hold the circle (which changes to red) to take a video.

After taking a photo or video, a large range of *filters* is displayed below the image. These emphasise different colours.

The spanner icon, as shown on the right, opens a set of editing tools, as shown on the right below.

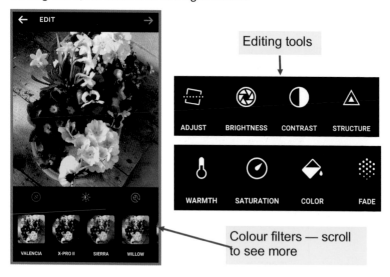

After editing, tap the arrow at the top right of the screen to write a caption for the photo, share on social networks or post it to your followers. The photos you've taken are saved in the **GALLERY**, listed at the top of this page. You can also import photos into Instagram which were previously stored on your Android device.

Creating and Printing Documents

Google Drive

This app brings all the advantages of *cloud computing* to Android smartphones and tablets. Suppose you use several computers at different times, such as your smartphone or tablet and perhaps a laptop or desktop machine. In the past, if you produced a document on one machine you would need to use one of the following methods to transfer it to another computer to carry on working.

- Transfer the files using a removable storage medium, such as a flash drive or CD, etc.
- E-mail the files to yourself as attachments.
- Copy the files across a home network. This requires both computers to be up and running simultaneously.

Using Google Drive, a file or document you save on one machine is automatically *synced* (*synchronised*) to all your other machines, via the *clouds*. The Google Drive app is free from the Play Store, discussed in Chapter 3. Google drive is then opened by tapping its icon on the apps screen, as shown on the right.

You can also download and install the free Google Drive application on any laptop and desktop computers which you use, as discussed shortly.

A Google Drive folder is created on each device on which you install Google Drive. New and edited files saved in a Drive folder are synced to the Drive folders on any other computers you use — smartphones, tablets, laptops and desktops. Google Drive has the following advantages:

- If you always save your files to the Drive folder, all your computers always have the latest editions.

- Your files are professionally managed on Google's server computers "in the clouds". However, if you delete a file from Google Drive, it may no longer be accessible to any of your computers. So I always back up important files to a hard drive, flash drive, etc.

- If you log on with your Gmail password, you can access your files from anywhere in the world.

- Colleagues and friends can collaborate, editing the same document on different machines.

Putting a Google Drive Folder on a Laptop or Desktop

Log on to **www.google.co.uk** on the laptop or desktop machine. Then select the **Apps** icon on the top right of the screen, shown here on the right. From the drop-down window which appears, select the **Drive** icon, shown on the right, to open the window shown below. Then click **Download Google Drive for PC** as shown on the blue button on the left below.

Drive

Google Docs

Once you've installed Google Drive you immediately have access to Google Docs, which is free *web-based software* and includes very capable word processing and spreadsheet apps. So this software will also be available on any computer with Google Drive installed, after you've signed in with your Gmail username and password.

If you want to write a 300 page novel you'd probably want to use a dedicated publishing program on a laptop or desktop computer. However, the tablet or smartphone is very useful for creating small documents and notes on the move. Also there are lots of accessories, discussed in Chapter 9, to convert a tablet or smartphone into a laptop/desktop replacement machine.

Creating a New Document

Tap the Drive icon on the Apps screen, shown on the right, to open the **My Drive** screen. Tap the red **Create** icon, shown on the lower right, to open the **New** window shown below, to start work on a new document.

Scan launches the camera on the tablet or smartphone, allowing you to scan a document and **Upload** is used to send a copy to the Google Drive cloud storage.

> Google Drive provides 15 GB of free storage in the clouds, for your files such as photos and documents, Gmail, etc.

Word Processing Using Google Docs

Tap Google Docs shown near the bottom of the previous page to open a new blank word processing page. Tap anywhere on the text area and start entering the text of your document.

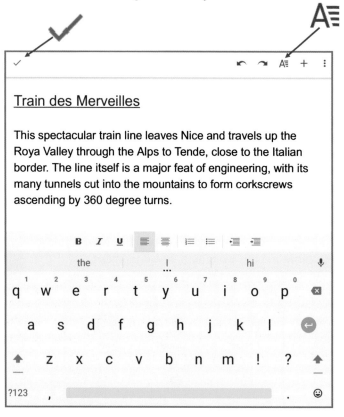

As shown above, there are all the usual word processing effects such as bold, italics and underline, bullets and justification, etc. Tapping the icon shown on the right and above displays options to change the font size, style and colour, etc.

Tap and hold a word to mark it ready for formatting and to display the menu shown below.

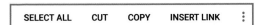

When you've finished entering and editing the text, tap the tick at the top left of the screen shown on the previous page. The document is automatically saved as **Untitled document** in Google Drive in the Clouds.

Tap **Untitled document** shown above to give your document a suitable name, as shown below, or accept the name suggested.

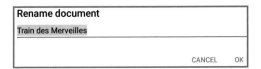

Rename document

Train des Merveilles

CANCEL   OK

Synchronisation Between Computers

The document is synced to your other computers and you can open it on them as soon as you sign into Gmail and open the Drive folder. The Train des Merveilles note created on a tablet, is shown below, synced to a PC. It also syncs to any other PCs, smartphones and tablets with your Google Drive account.

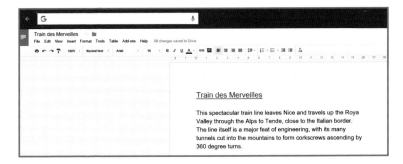

Using the Google Docs Spreadsheet

Tap the Google Drive icon and then tap the **Create** button as shown on page 131. Then tap **Google** Sheets, also shown on page 131.

A blank spreadsheet opens ready for you to start entering the data, as shown below.

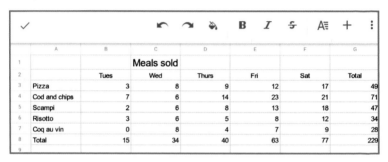

	A	B	C	D	E	F	G
1			Meals sold				
2		Tues	Wed	Thurs	Fri	Sat	Total
3	Pizza	3	8	9	12	17	49
4	Cod and chips	7	6	14	23	21	71
5	Scampi	2	6	8	13	18	47
6	Risotto	3	6	5	8	12	34
7	Coq au vin	0	8	4	7	9	28
8	Total	15	34	40	63	77	229
9							

It may be more convenient to hold a smartphone or small tablet in landscape mode to display a large spreadsheet. If necessary, in order to display landscape view, swipe down from the top right of the screen and make sure **AUTO ROTATE** appears in the Quick Settings panel, not **ROTATION LOCKED**, as discussed on page 64.

This enables you to see all of the icons on the menu bar across the top of the screen, without having to scroll horizontally. Tap to select a cell, such as **G8**. Then use the keyboard to enter or edit numbers, text or a formula, after tapping in the bar at the bottom of the sheet, shown below displaying a formula.

fx =SUM(B8:F8)   ‹   ›

Tap the icons shown on the right to switch between text and numbers on the on-screen keyboard. These icons appear just above the keyboard on the right.

As shown on the previous page, the spreadsheet app has the normal text formatting tools, such as undo, redo, bold, italic, underline, etc., and text in various fonts, sizes and colours. Columns or rows can be selected for editing by tapping at the top of a column or at the extreme left of a row. Tap the tick at the top left of the sheet to save the spreadsheet in the clouds. A spreadsheet can be given a name in the same way as a Google Docs word processing document, as described on page 133.

Managing Your Files in Google Drive

The word processing and spreadsheet docs that you create are saved in the clouds as files on a Google server computer. The files are listed on the **My Drive** page on the Android smartphone or tablet, when you first sign into **Gmail** and launch **Drive**. To fully open a particular file, tap its thumbnail, as shown below.

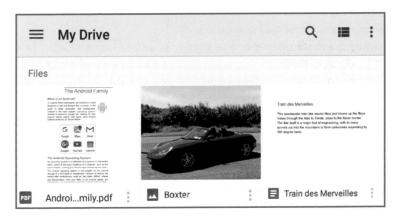

As shown above, **My Drive** in this example displays the thumbnails representing various types of file. On the left is the **.pdf** file for the first chapter of this book. This was created on a desktop PC and synced automatically to my smartphones and tablets via the clouds. The middle file is a photo in the standard **.jpeg** format (*Joint Photographic Experts Group*). On the right is the train document created on an Android tablet.

Tap the 3-dot menu button below a file's thumbnail in **My Drive**, as shown on the right for a photo. You are presented with the following menu, including common options to **Remove**, **Rename** and **Print** the file.

You can also send a copy of a file or a link to a file to various destinations such as Gmail, Twitter, Facebook and Dropbox, for example.

Boxter

Viewing Files Offline

Normally files saved in Google Drive exist only in the "clouds", i.e. on the Internet server computers of Google, Inc. So to view them you need to be *online*, i.e. connected to the Internet. To make files available for viewing *offline*, where there is no Internet connection switch **Available offline ON** by tapping the button to slide it to the right, as shown below.

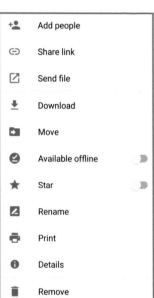

Add people

Share link

Send file

Download

Move

Available offline

Star

Rename

Print

Details

Remove

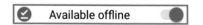

Available offline

For entering a lot of text or numbers, you can use a separate physical keyboard, as mentioned in Chapter 9. Alternatively, tap the microphone icon on the on-screen keyboard and *speak* the data.

Microsoft Office for Android

Microsoft have dominated the business world for many years with their leading Office software suite including the word processor MS Word and the Excel spreadsheet. Now these leading products are available for Android tablets and smartphones together with the PowerPoint presentation app, the Outlook e-mail and calendar and the OneNote digital notebook.

These apps, including OneDrive, are all free from the Play Store shown below and can be installed as discussed in Chapter 3.

Launching the MS Office Apps

After the Office apps are installed, their icons appear on the Apps screen. Or you might want to copy them to a vacant space on the Home screen, as shown below and discussed in Chapter 3. Tap the icon to launch an app, such as Word.

Alternatively you could group the apps into a folder, such as Office 365, as discussed in Chapter 3.

Office 365 folder icon

Office 365 folder contents

OneDrive

This is Microsoft's cloud storage system which enables files such as Word processing documents to be synced to all your computers. OneDrive provides 5GB of free storage in the clouds for your photos and files — very useful if the Internal Storage on your smartphone or tablet is getting full. OneDrive is similar to Google Drive and Dropbox discussed elsewhere in this book.

MS Word on Android Tablets and Smartphones

Although originally designed for desktop computers, the Word app has a very similar look and feel on an Android tablet, with the main formatting features still present, as shown below (approximately half size).

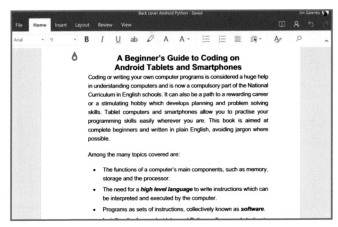

Microsoft Word on an Android tablet

The Word document is still quite readable on an Android smartphone in landscape mode and again the essential editing tools are still present as shown below (approximately full size).

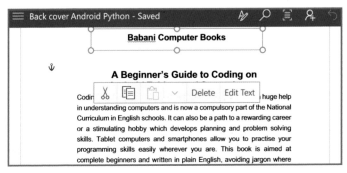

Microsoft Word on an Android smartphone

Excel and PowerPoint on Android

Shown below are Android screenshots from the leading spreadsheet Microsoft Excel and the PowerPoint presentation app. These files were produced on a PC desktop computer and imported into an Android tablet where they can be viewed and edited "on the move".

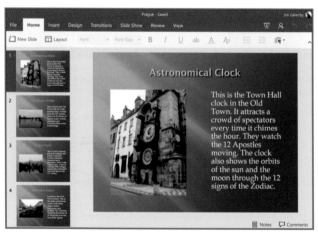

An Excel spreadsheet on an Android tablet

A PowerPoint presentation on an Android tablet

One of the main advantages of having important MS Office apps such as Word, Excel and PowerPoint on a tablet or smartphone is that documents can be created, viewed and edited away from your home or office. The files are completely compatible with Android devices and PC laptop and desktop machines, so you can carry on working on the same document wherever you are.

If necessary, a tablet or smartphone can be connected to a large HDMI screen or projector, for example to illustrate a talk or PowerPoint slide show presentation.

Saving to OneDrive

After installing the OneDrive app from the Play Store, as discussed in Chapter 3, you need to sign in to a Microsoft account or create a new one.

Saving Word and Excel Files to One Drive Automatically

Make sure **Auto Save** is switched **On**, in the **Save** option as shown below.

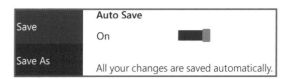

To view your files on OneDrive in the clouds, i.e. on the Internet, tap the OneDrive icon shown on the right.

Saving Photos Automatically to OneDrive

To automatically save *photos* to OneDrive, open OneDrive by tapping its icon on the Apps screen, then tap **Settings** at the bottom of the screen and make sure **Camera upload** is **On**.

Saving on the Internal Storage of Your Device

In Word or Excel, use the **Save as** option to **Browse** to one of the folders on your device to save a file on the Internal Storage.

Google Cloud Printing
Setting Up a Cloud Printer

Google Cloud Print is an app which allows any computer, such as an Android tablet or smartphone to print documents across the Web to any printer, anywhere. Cloud Print is a free app in the Google Play Store and can be installed as discussed in Chapter 3.

If you already have a *cloud ready* (Wi-Fi) printer which connects to the Web without being attached to a computer, this should be easy to set up using the manufacturer's instructions.

A printer which is not cloud ready (i.e. not a Wi-Fi printer), is referred to as a *classic* printer. The classic printer must be connected by a cable to a laptop or desktop computer on a *Wi-Fi network with a router*. The computer must have Google Chrome installed in order to set up the Cloud Print service as discussed below.

Open Google Chrome and make sure you are signed in with your Gmail address and password. Tap the Chrome menu button shown on the right and below and from the menu select **Settings**. Then scroll down the screen and at the bottom select **Show advanced settings**. Scroll down the next screen and under **Google Cloud Print** select **Manage** and then select the printer you wish to use.

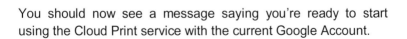

You should now see a message saying you're ready to start using the Cloud Print service with the current Google Account.

This will enable you to print wirelessly from an Android tablet or smartphone from anywhere in the home, etc..

Cloud Printing from an Android Device

Open the main Android **Settings** screen as discussed in Chapter 4 and select **Printing**. You should see the **Cloud Print** service.

Tap **Cloud Print** shown above and you should see the name of your printer, as shown below. If necessary tap the green button to switch the printing service **On**.

Cloud Printing a Document from Google Drive

To print a document in Google Drive using Cloud Print, tap the 3-dot menu button at the bottom right of the thumbnail for the document in Google Drive, as shown below.

From the menu which appears, select **Print**, as shown in the extract on the right. This opens the **Cloud Print** window on the tablet or smartphone, as shown below.

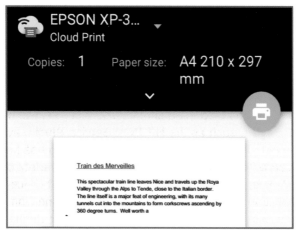

The Cloud Print window shown above includes drop-down options to select a different Cloud Printer, specify the number of copies and change the paper size, orientation (portrait or landscape) and either colour or black and white.

To print the document, tap the icon shown on the right and above.

Cloud Printing from MS Office for Android

Using the Android versions of MS Office apps, i.e. Word, Excel and PowerPoint, select **File** and **Print** from the ribbon across the top of the screen. The Cloud Print window opens, as shown above, ready for you print the document after changing any settings, if necessary.

Printing Without a Router

The previous pages described cloud printing in which your smartphone or tablet is connected to a printer on a Wi-Fi network via a router. It's also possible to print from a smartphone or tablet *directly* to certain printers, without involving a router. Several HP printers are suitable for direct printing, including the HP Deskjet 2540, (currently available for under £50) which is designed for use with smartphones and tablets. The advantage of direct printing is that you can print in places where there is no Internet.

In this form of *direct printing* the Wi-Fi printer is detected using the Wi-Fi of the smartphone or tablet and connected in the same way as a router, as discussed shortly. You also need to connect to a *print service*, such as the **HP Print Service Plugin**, available as an app from the Play Store. Once direct printing has been set up, you can print documents and photos from a variety of apps such as Photos, Gmail, Google Drive and Microsoft Office. Since your connection to the printer *replaces* your connection to the router, you will not be connected to the Internet during direct printing. So any files to be printed need to be first downloaded and saved on your device while still connected to the Internet and before connecting the printer.

Setting Up Direct Printing

- On the printer, make sure the HP Wireless Direct Printing light is on, as shown on the right. Press the HP Wireless Direct Printing button if necessary. A list of instructions is printed, including a *password* for the printer.

- Turn on **Wi-Fi** in **Settings** on your smartphone or tablet.

- Tap the **HP Deskjet 2540** printer in the list of devices (mainly routers) which appears and select **CONNECT**.

- Enter the *password* for the printer, as mentioned above. The printer should now be connected as shown below.

- Install the **HP Print Service Plugin** app from the Google Play Store.

- In the main Android **Settings** screen tap **Printing** then tap **HP Print Service Plugin**.

- Make sure **HP Print Service Plugin** is **On** and **HP Deskjet 2540** printer is listed, as shown below.

- You are now ready to start printing from apps such as Google Drive, etc., as discussed on the previous pages.

HP ePrint

This is a cloud printing service developed by Hewlett-Packard, for use with smartphones, tablet computers and laptops, etc.. A free *HP ePrint* app is available in the Play Store. The system requires an HP ePrint compatible Wi-Fi printer registered to the HP ePrint cloud service called *HP ePrint Center*. This assigns a unique e-mail address to the printer.

The document to be printed is attached to an e-mail sent to the e-mail address of the ePrinter. Documents can be printed in many of the well-known file formats, such as MS Word, PowerPoint, JPEG, PDF and HTML, etc. Microsoft Office documents need to be processed at the HP ePrint Center.

Printing Over a Home or Local Wi-Fi Network

HP ePrint can be used to print wirelessly from an Android tablet or smartphone. In the home or small business situation this requires an ePrint compatible printer connected to the Internet via Wi-Fi or by a USB cable to a laptop or desktop computer. Most HP printers are compatible with ePrint, including the inexpensive HP Deskjet 2540 shown on page 145.

Using ePrinters in Public Locations

HP ePrint can also be used by people on the move who need to print while away from the home or office. This uses a number of *HP ePrint Public Print* locations. These are public printers located, for example, in hotels and airports, etc. These allow the users of a smartphone or tablet to print documents (for a fee) while travelling. HP ePrint uses GPS to list a number of hotels, etc., providing public printing facilities in a particular area.

HP ePrint Enterprise

This is designed for large organisations such as businesses and academic institutions, to allow staff to print from mobile devices when travelling between various offices, etc.

Using HP ePrint on a Wi-Fi Network

The ePrinter must be set up and connected to the Internet. Install the free ePrint app from the Play Store, as shown on the right, as discussed in Chapter 3. Tap the ePrint icon on the Apps screen and then tap **Activate Now**. Enter your e-mail address, tap **Activate** at the top right of the window and you will be sent an e-mail containing a 4-character activation code. Enter the code and tap **Activate** at the top right of the Activate window.

You should then receive congratulations and after tapping **Done** you will be ready to start printing **Photos**, **Files**, **Web** pages and **Emails** from your Android smartphone or tablet. Select a category such as **Files** then browse your Android **Device Storage** for the file to be printed, as shown on the right below.

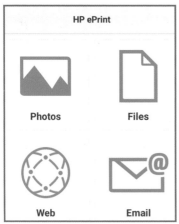
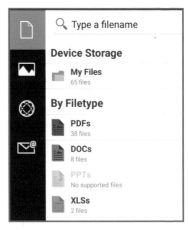

Then select **Preview** and check your printer is selected, before tapping the **Print** button, shown below.

Managing Your Android

Introduction

A document, image, photograph or video clip, etc., saved on a computer storage medium, is known as a *file*. There are many different *file formats*, depending on the app or program which has created the file. Some common file formats include *JPEG (Joint Photographic Experts Group)* used for photos and images and *PDF (Portable Display Format)* used for text documents. Files saved in these formats can be opened and viewed on most computers, including Android tablets and smartphones. Less common formats may not be compatible with Android devices, although there may be an app in the Play Store which can be used to open the file.

You may often need to transfer files between an Android tablet or smartphone and other computers and storage devices. Some methods for transferring files are as follows:

- Connect an OTG (On The Go) cable to the Micro USB port on the Android. This can be used to connect USB devices such as a card reader, flash drive, etc.

- Use a laptop or desktop computer to manage the Android's files via a USB cable.

- Use a cloud storage system such as Google Drive, OneDrive or *Dropbox*.

- Use the Micro SD card slot available on many tablets and smartphones. Manage the files on the Micro SD card with an app such as ES File Explorer.

Google Drive and OneDrive were discussed in the last chapter. The other methods above are discussed later in this chapter.

Useful Accessories

The following may be helpful when transferring files between an Android tablet or smartphone and other devices such as a laptop or desktop PC or an Apple computer. You will also need the Android battery charger cable to connect the tablet or smartphone to another computer.

OTG Cable

This connects the Micro USB port on an Android to a full-size USB female port, allowing various USB devices such as an SD card reader, flash drive, mouse, keyboard and digital camera to be connected.

The OTG cable

USB Flash Drive

Also known as a *memory stick*, this can be connected to the OTG cable for the transfer of files to and from the Android tablet or smartphone.

USB flash drive

USB Card Reader

These can take SD cards such as those from a camera, for importing photos to an Android device. It can also be used by the Android for saving files. Laptop computers and printers often have a built-in card reader.

USB SD card reader

Micro SD Adaptor

Some Androids have a Micro SD slot, allowing a card to be inserted. Files saved on the Micro SD card in an Android device can be transferred to a PC computer after inserting the Micro SD card into the adaptor. The adaptor fits into a slot in an SD card reader, which may be built into a laptop or desktop PC or printer. Micro SD cards are available from 4GB up to 128GB.

Micro SD adaptor and card

Mobile High Definition Link (MHL)

This is a system developed by leading manufacturers such as Samsung, Sony and Toshiba to allow the output from an MHL-compatible Android tablet or smartphone to be displayed on an HDMI television. A cable or adapter is used to connect the microUSB port on the Android to the HDMI port on the television.

Chromecast

The **Chromecast** is a thumb-sized *dongle* which plugs into a port on an HDMI television. Then videos, web pages, photos etc., on the tablet or smartphone can be viewed on a TV screen.

The input source on the TV should be set to HDMI.

Install the Chromecast app from the Play store, as discussed in Chapter 3. Then open the required photo or video, etc. The Cast button appears at the top right of the Android screen, as shown on the right and below. Tap the Cast button to mirror the Android screen to the TV screen.

Chromecast

A **Cast** button also appears on **Quick Settings** shown on page 64.

Expanding an Android Tablet

There are various ways to convert an Android tablet into a replacement for a laptop or desktop computer. As mentioned on page 151, there are cables and adapters which allow a tablet to be connected to an HDMI monitor, TV or projector.

The OTG cable shown on page 150 can be used to connect a *USB multi-port hub*, as shown on the right, to which you can attach several devices such as a USB mouse and keyboard. Or you can insert a *USB wireless dongle* into the OTG cable and use this to power a *wireless keyboard* and *mouse*.

Bluetooth

Android tablets generally have their own built-in, short-range wireless technology, known as *Bluetooth*. This can be used to connect devices such as a keyboard, mouse and printer, for working on long documents, etc. Bluetooth avoids the need for USB cables or dongles, as mentioned above.

Pairing Two Bluetooth Devices

To connect a Bluetooth device, such as a keyboard or mouse, to an Android tablet or smartphone, the two devices have to be *paired* as follows. On the Android, open the **Quick Settings** window as described on page 64 and 65, select **SETTINGS** and make sure **Bluetooth** is **ON**, as shown at the top of the next page. In this example, **XT1068** is a Moto G smartphone. Make sure the Bluetooth keyboard is switched **ON** and press the **Connect** button on the keyboard. A blue light should flash.

Any Bluetooth devices near to the Android tablet or smartphone, such as the **Bluetooth keyboard**, are listed under **Available devices**, as shown at the top of the next page.

Tap the name of the device, **Bluetooth Keyboard** in this example, to start the pairing process, as shown below. You may see one (or sometimes two) pairing codes displayed as shown on the left, before tapping **PAIR** to start the pairing process.

Finally, the **Bluetooth Keyboard** is listed as **Connected** under **Paired devices** and is now ready to be used with your Android tablet or smartphone.

It's often recommended that Bluetooth is switched off when not in use. There is some debate that Bluetooth causes the battery of the tablet or smartphone to be drained quickly.

Using the Micro USB Port

The *Micro USB* port built into the Android tablets and smartphones and shown on page 16 can easily be converted to a full-size standard USB port using an OTG (On The Go) cable, as shown on page 150.

The OTG cable can be used for connecting USB devices (as indicated below) to an Android device for importing of files.

- A standard SD card in a USB card reader.
- A USB flash drive/memory stick.
- A separate digital camera.

Importing Photos from a USB Device

The Nexus Media Importer app is free and can be downloaded and installed from the Play Store as discussed in Chapter 3. Connect the USB device to the smartphone or tablet using the OTG cable. The USB device is detected and in response to **Choose an app for the USB device**, tap **Nexus Media Importer**. Then tap **OK**, as shown below, to allow the Nexus Media Importer to access the USB device.

1. Nexus Media Importer
Homesoft
★ ★ ★ ★ ✦

Nexus Media Importer

Allow the app Nexus Media Importer to access the USB device?

☐ Use by default for this USB device

Tap **All Photos** or **Folders** to open thumbnails of the photos on the device, as shown at the top of the next page.

All Photos   Folders

Viewing Photos Stored on an SD Card, etc.

To view a large version of a photo on the SD card or flash drive, double tap a thumbnail, as shown above. You may wish to keep your photo collection on separate SD cards and always view them from the storage medium in this way.

Copying Photos to the Internal Storage

If you wish to save copies of photos on the internal storage of the tablet or smartphone, tap a thumbnail to display the tool icons shown below and on the top right above.

 Saves a **Copy** of the photo on the internal storage of the Android device in the **Pictures** folder, discussed shortly.

 The **Move** button saves a photo in the **Pictures** folder on the internal storage and deletes the original image from the SD card, or flash drive, etc.

 The **Delete** button removes photos from a USB storage medium such as an SD card or flash drive, etc.

 Use the **Share** button to send copies of photos to e-mail, **Photos**, Facebook, Twitter, Dropbox, Google Drive, etc.

 This **Menu** button has options including **Edit, Slide Show** and **Rotate,** etc.

Managing an Android Device from a PC

In addition to Android apps such as the Nexus Media Importer and ES File Explorer, you can use a Windows PC to manage the files on an Android tablet or smartphone. Connect the Android to the PC using the Android USB charging cable. The Android, in this example a Nexus 7 tablet, appears like a disc drive or flash drive in File Explorer on the PC, (previously known as Windows Explorer).

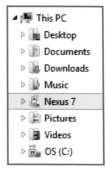

The extract on the right shows the **Nexus 7** listed on a laptop computer in the File Explorer in Windows 10. Double-clicking the name **Nexus 7** in the list displays the **Internal storage** of the Nexus 7, as if it's another disc drive, here showing **23.9GB** free out of a maximum of **27.5GB**.

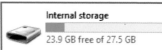

Double-clicking on the **Internal storage** image above displays all the folders on the tablet or smartphone. Double-click a folder to view the files within, such as the **Pictures** folder listed below.

▶ **This PC** ▶ **Nexus 7** ▶ **Internal storage** ▶ **Pictures**

Right-click a file in the File Explorer window to open the menu shown on the right. This includes options to use the PC to **Delete**, **Edit**, **Copy** and **Rename** files. Files can be copied to and from the Android, by dragging and dropping or copying and pasting using the Windows File Explorer.

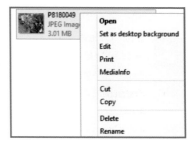

Dropbox

Dropbox is a very popular cloud storage system and an alternative to Google Drive, discussed in Chapter 8. Dropbox has millions of users, both private individuals and businesses. Dropbox initially provides you with 2GB of free storage space on an Internet server, but more is available for a monthly premium.

Your Android tablet or smartphone may already have Dropbox installed with an icon on the Apps screen as shown on the right. If not you can easily download and install the Dropbox app from the Play Store, as discussed in Chapter 3. Then sign up to Dropbox with an e-mail address and password.

If you have laptop and desktop machines, you can download Dropbox to all of them from the Web site:

www.dropbox.com

The essential features of Dropbox are:

- A Dropbox folder must be placed on all the computers on which you wish to share files.

- You must be signed in with your Dropbox e-mail address and password.

- Save or copy your files to the Dropbox folder.

- Latest copies of files are copied to the Dropbox Web server computers then synced to all your computers.

- Your files can then be accessed on any computer with a Dropbox folder which you are signed into - tablet, laptop, desktop, iPad, etc.

- Important files should still be backed up on *local media* such as hard drives and flash drives. With an Android this can be done by connecting to a PC as discussed earlier. (Some Androids can also copy files to a Micro SD card as discussed on the next page).

Using a Micro SD Card

Android tablets and smartphones typically have 16GB to 64GB (gigabytes) of Internal Storage on which to save your photos, music, videos and documents, etc. For extra local storage, some tablets and smartphones have a slot for a *Micro SD card* as shown on page 151, which can add another 64GB, 128GB or even 200GB.

From the **Settings** menu select **Storage** and scroll down and tap **Mount SD card**. Then tap **Format SD card**. Formatting prepares a new card or wipes files from a used card.

You can use an app like the *Nexus Media Importer* discussed on page 156 or *ES File Explorer*, available free from the Play Store, to copy, delete and generally manage the files on a Micro SD card. Alternatively, to manage the files on a Micro SD card, you can use a PC, as discussed on page 156.

Samsung Galaxy

Samsung Galaxy tablets and smartphones such as the S5 and S7 have a slot for a Micro SD card inside of the back cover. From the **Settings** menu, tap **Mount** and, if necessary, **Format** the Micro SD card as described above.

Moving Apps to the SD Card

To move apps to the SD card, in the main **Settings,** under **Applications**, tap **Application manager**. Then select the application and under **Storage** tap **MOVE TO SD CARD**.

Moving Files to the SD Card

Open **My Files** on the **Apps** screen, then under **Local Storage** tap **Device Storage**. Then browse to find the files to be moved, open the 3-dot menu, tap **Select** and then tap to tick the files to be moved. Then select **Move** and **SD card**. Finally select **MOVE HERE**. There is an option in the **Camera** app settings to set the **SD card** to be the default storage location for new photos.

Cameras on an Android Device

Android tablets and smartphones have both forward and backward facing cameras, making it easier to take various photos and videos of people and objects. Although the screen layouts and icons may vary, the general methods for taking photos on Android devices are as follows.

To take a general photograph looking in front of you, tap the icon shown on the right, on the Apps screen. This opens the camera on the back of the tablet or smartphone. Tap anywhere on the screen, or on Samsung devices tap the camera icon, to take a photo.

The icon shown on the right allows you to switch from photo to video mode. Tap the square icon shown on the lower right to stop recording the video. The camera then returns to photo mode.

The icon shown on the right allows you to switch between the rear camera for taking normal phots and the front camera for taking "selfies".

Viewing Photos

Thumbnails of the photos and videos taken with an Android tablet or phone can now be viewed after tapping the **Photos** icon, shown on the right.

Photos

Tap to open a photo, then tap the 3-dot menu button shown on the right. This displays options including **Details**, **Print** and **Edit in**.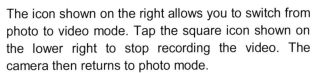

Tap an open photo to display the menu bar across the bottom of the screen, as shown below. Reading form left to right, this has options to share, edit, view information or delete the photo.

Sharing Photos

Tapping the sharing icon shown on the right and on the previous page allows you to send photos, etc., to a variety of destinations, as shown in the small sample below.

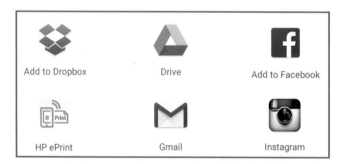

Add to Dropbox   Drive   Add to Facebook

HP ePrint   Gmail   Instagram

Editing Photos

Tap the icon shown on the right and on the previous page to display some photo editing tools, shown below.

Auto   Light   Colour   Pop   Vignette

Capturing a Screenshot

To send a copy of a screen to a friend or to include in an article, report, etc., you can capture the Android screen as follows.

Simultaneously hold down the **Power** button and the **Volume** button (at the *volume down* end). The screenshot can then be viewed as a **.PNG** file in the **Photos** app as described above, or sent using the sharing button shown at the top of the page on the right.

Security

The Android O.S. has a number of security features within the **Security** section of **Settings**, described on pages 67 and 68. These are designed to prevent "hackers" trying to steal money or private information or cause inconvenience.

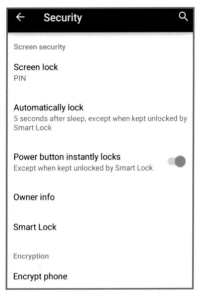

Various options for the screen lock prevent other people from using your smartphone or tablet when it first starts up or after sleep mode. Tap **Screen lock** shown above, then choose from creating a **Pattern**, or entering a **PIN** or a **Password** in addition to the default setting to swipe a padlock icon. A *facial recognition* option appears after you've set one of the other options such as **Pattern**, **PIN** or **Password**.

Encryption shown above scrambles all the data on your tablet or phone. It can only be deciphered by someone knowing your **PIN** or **Password**, etc. On the negative side, encryption can slow a computer's performance. Also, to cancel the encryption you need to reset the computer to its original factory settings.

Further Security Precautions

- In the **Security** section of **Settings** make sure **Unknown sources** is **OFF**. This will not allow rogue software, which may contain viruses, to be installed. Then only genuine apps from the Play Store can be installed.

Unknown sources
Allow installation of apps from sources other than the Play Store

---

- Choose obscure passwords and change them regularly.

- Do not give passwords, credit card or account details in reply to e-mails or telephone calls.

- If you forget your password you can usually reset it by tapping **Forgot password?** A *link to a Web site* will be e-mailed to you, allowing you to reset the password.

- Always make multiple backup copies of important files or valuable photos. These may be on professionally managed *cloud storage systems* such as Google Drive, Dropbox or Microsoft OneDrive.

- Also make backup copies on separate removable media such as *flash drives* or on other computers such as PC desktops and laptops, as discussed earlier.

- A stolen smartphone can be located using one of the *tracking apps* from the Play Store. A code is sent by text to the phone, which rings. Another code is sent back to you giving the GPS coordinates of the stolen phone.

- Set Parental Controls, where available, to control what apps or Web sites your children can access. As discussed on page 42, you can also set a *PIN* to prevent anyone spending a lot of money on *In app purchases*.

Further Connections

Introduction

The Internet is a network of millions of computers linked by broadband telephone cables, wireless radio waves and satellite communications.

Many people will connect to the Internet via a *router* in their home, place of work, school, college or *wireless hotspot*. However, there may be times when you don't have any access to Wi-Fi such as on holiday or working in a remote place. Or perhaps your router may develop a technical fault or your broadband telephone landline may be temporarily out of action.

This chapter includes the following topics:

- Connecting to the Internet using a wireless router in the home or a wireless hotspot in the wider community.

- Accessing the Internet via a *cell phone network* using 3G/4G smartphones and 3G/4G enabled tablets.

- The different types of Internet *data* and explanations of various terms such as *megabyte* and *gigabyte*.

- Using a smartphone as a *mobile hotspot* for *tethering Wi-Fi only* tablets to connect to the Internet.

- Using an Android device as a *Sat Nav* with Google Maps and a *GPS* (Global Positioning System) .

- Downloading Google maps from the Internet for use *offline*, i.e. where there is no Internet.

- Scanning QR bar codes to connect easily to Web sites.

Wi-Fi Connections

This is the usual way for the home user to connect to the Internet, whether using a smartphone tablet, laptop or desktop computer. You need to sign up for an account with an *Internet Service Provider* (*ISP*) such as BT, Sky, Virgin, TalkTalk or EE. A new account may include a free *wireless router*, a small plastic box which plugs into a *broadband* telephone socket in your home. Smartphones, tablets and laptops normally have a built-in *Wi-Fi adapter* to communicate wirelessly with the router.

Several tablets or smartphones can communicate wirelessly around a typical house or flat via a router, but the signal strength deteriorates with distance and obstructions such as brick walls.

There are now many other Wi-Fi Internet *access points* around the UK, many of them free to use. These *wireless hotspots* are found in hotels, cafes, airports, railway stations and even on trains and buses. BT have millions of hotspots around the UK.

Key Points: Wi-Fi Internet Access

- You need to be within range (perhaps 100-150 feet) of a Wi-Fi router or hotspot, depending on obstructions.

- The router connects to the Internet via a cabled network such as BT Broadband using copper or fibre cables.

- For a home router you need an account with an ISP, as mentioned above, costing perhaps £20-£30 a month.

- Wi-Fi provided via an external hotspot in a public place such as a cafe or hotel is generally free.

- A *Wi-Fi only* tablet costs less than a *3G/4G tablet*. A 3G/4G tablet can connect to a cell phone network.

- Many Wi-Fi broadband networks, often using a router in the home, allow *unlimited downloads* of data.

3G and 4G Connections

3G and 4G systems connect to the Internet using radio waves between networks of cell phone (i.e. mobile phone) towers around the UK. Smartphones have built-in 3G or 4G capability, of which 4G (*4th generation*) is the latest and fastest. If you need to use the Internet on the move where there are no routers or wireless hotspots, smartphones and 3G/4G tablets are a solution.

Smartphones

As well as normal voice and text messaging, smartphones can be used for Internet activities like e-mail, social networking, downloading music or video and browsing the Worldwide Web. However, for these Internet activities you need a *data plan* with a cell phone network such as EE or TalkTalk, etc.

3G/4G Tablets

Unlike *Wi-Fi only* tablets, 3G/4G tablets connect to the Internet using a cell phone network and a data plan.

Key Points: Smartphones and 3G/4G Tablets

- Can connect to the Internet wherever there is a cell phone, i.e. mobile phone, signal.

- Require a data plan with a cell phone network.

- Can also be used with a W-Fi router, e.g. on a home network, in addition to a 3G or 4G cell phone network.

- It's cheaper to use Wi-Fi whenever possible, either using a home router or wireless hotspot.

- The 3G/4G tablet costs considerably more than the Wi-Fi only version of the same tablet — perhaps £100 more.

- **Mobile data** needs to be switched **ON** in **Settings**.

Data

This is the "traffic" which is *downloaded* from the Internet to your smartphone or tablet, or *uploaded* from your device to the Internet. Most of your data will probably be downloaded but some traffic will be uploaded, such as the e-mails you send and any files you include as *attachments*. Typical downloaded files would be Web pages, music, video and television programmes.

Cloud computing, discussed earlier, involves uploading and downloading files you create, such as documents and photos.

Common units used to measure data are the *megabyte* and *gigabyte* as discussed below.

Byte	A group of 8 binary digits (0s and 1s) or bits. A byte may be used to represent a digit 0-9, a letter, punctuation mark or keyboard character, for example.
Kilobyte (KB):	1024 bytes
Megabyte (MB):	1024KB
Gigabyte (GB):	1024MB
Terabyte (TB):	1024GB

If you have a contract allowing you unlimited data, you needn't worry too much about the cost of your Internet activities. However, some Internet Service Providers and cell phone companies include a data plan with a fixed limit. If you exceed your limit you will be charged for the extra data over the limit.

As a rough guide, the average Web page is about 1MB while a photo could be 1-5MB. Activities such as downloading and watching videos and TV programmes are heavy users of data. Streaming a 90 minute video might use 1GB of data.

Mobile Data

To use a smartphone or a 3G/4G tablet to connect to the Internet where there is no Wi-Fi, you need to switch **Mobile data ON**. Open **Settings**, as discussed on page 67 and 68 and select **Data usage** in the **Wireless & networks** section. Then tap or slide the button to switch **Mobile data ON**, as shown below. This will enable you to connect to the Internet via your cell phone network and use the full range of activities such as sending and receiving e-mails and downloading music, video, books and maps, etc.

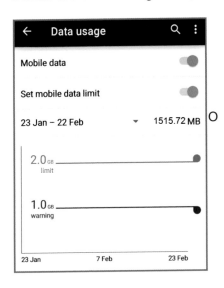

Always use Wi-Fi when possible and switch **Mobile data OFF** when it's not needed.

You can drag the black slider shown above to set a *warning notification* when you've used a certain amount of data. The red slider is used to specify a *limit* to how much data you can use before your mobile data use is terminated. 2GB per month is probably more than enough for most users. Some cell phone networks allow *unlimited data* while others make a charge, such as £15 for 500MB of data.

Exceeding your data plan can be expensive

Tethering – Setting Up a Mobile Hotspot

Tethering allows a Wi-Fi only tablet (or laptop) to connect to the Internet in a place where there is no Wi-Fi. The Wi-Fi only device connects wirelessly to a smartphone and shares the 3G/4G Internet connection of the smartphone, which acts as a *mobile hotspot*. To connect a *laptop* to use the smartphone's Internet connection you need a *microUSB* to *USB* cable.

On the smartphone, make sure **Mobile data** is **ON** as discussed on page 167. Then under **Wireless & networks**, select **More** and **Tethering & mobile hotspot**. Next switch **Mobile Wi-Fi hotspot ON** and tap **Set up Wi-Fi hotspot**.

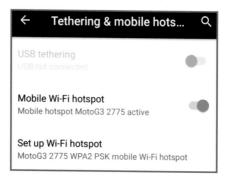

A name for the hotspot appears automatically and you then need to enter a password and save the settings.

Then your smartphone will appear on the Wi-Fi only tablet in the list of routers/hotspots you can connect to, as shown below and discussed in more detail on page 23.

Tethering a Wi-Fi only tablet to a smartphone

In an emergency, e.g. if your Wi-Fi router stops working, you could use a smartphone as a mobile hotspot to connect to the Internet. Due to the extra cost of 3G/4G compared with Wi-Fi, this would probably only be a temporary solution.

Saving Files for Off-line Use

If you're going away, perhaps on holiday, there may not be a good Wi-Fi hotspot in the new place. Before leaving home download any files you might need and save them on the Internal Storage of your smartphone or tablet. This will also be cheaper than using a 3G/4G cell phone network to download files in your new location. Typical files to download and save might be music, video, e-books, maps and data files. Downloading books for reading off-line is discussed on page 83.

Using an Android Device as a Sat Nav

Many Android smartphones and tablets now have a built-in *GPS* (Global Positioning System) *receiver*, as used in Sat Nav route navigating systems in cars, ships and aircraft, etc. This communicates with a system of satellites which orbit the earth. Your GPS receiver needs to be able to detect at least 4 satellites. Microwaves from the satellites are used to calculate your exact position *at any time*. This can then be used in Google Now, as discussed in Chapter 4, to display up-to-date information about your current location, such news, weather and traffic problems.

You don't need an Internet connection to use GPS.

Planning a Journey With Google Maps

This work is based on Google Maps. When you're using a smartphone or tablet on a Wi-Fi network via a broadband router, any maps you require from around the world can be downloaded from the Internet as required.

To use Google maps where there is no Wi-Fi you need to:

Use a smartphone or tablet with 3G/4G capability via a cell phone, i.e. mobile phone, network.

Or:

Download and save the maps you require before setting off, while you can still connect to Wi-Fi, as discussed shortly.

Launching Google Maps

Android smartphones and tablets have an icon for Google Maps already installed on the Apps screen, as shown on the right. When you first tap the **Maps** icon, it uses *GPS* to display a map of your current area. To find a map of another area, enter a *place name* or *post code* in the search bar, as shown on the next page.

Maps

For example, if you wanted to travel from your current location to Edinburgh, enter this destination in the Search Bar.

Stretch or pinch the map with two fingers to zoom in or zoom out to show the area you wish to see.

With a car or other motor vehicle selected as shown on the right, the time for the journey to Edinburgh from your current location would be 4 hours 53 minutes in this example.

Tap the vehicle icon shown on the previous page. The fastest route is displayed on the map as shown below. The 3-dot menu button shown below allows you to select *alternative routes* and to select a **Satellite** view. A listing of the major roads on the route is shown in the left-hand panel below.

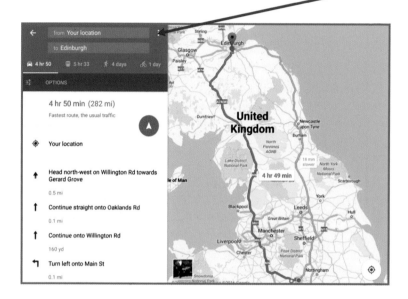

Options at the top left of the screen, shown above, allow you to select different modes of transport, such as motor vehicles, public transport, walking and cycling, as shown below.

Before Setting Off

Smartphone and 3G/4G Tablet

When you're ready to set off, if you're using a smartphone or tablet with 3G/4G connectivity to a mobile phone network you will need to make sure **Mobile data** is switched **ON** in **Settings** and **Data usage**, as discussed on page 167. This will enable the smartphone or 3G/4G tablet to download maps from the Internet as you are travelling.

Wi-Fi Only Tablet

If you're using a Wi-Fi only tablet, i.e. which can't connect to the Internet without a broadband router, you'll need to download and save the maps for your journey before leaving home, as discussed on the next page.

Starting the Journey

Tap the **Start** or **Navigate** icon as shown on the right and on the previous page. A live, constantly changing map of your route appears with spoken directions and the estimated time to reach your destination.

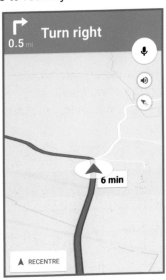

Downloading and Saving Maps for Use Offline

If you have a Wi-Fi only tablet, you can still use it as a Sat Nav, even without a connection to the Internet. You just need to download and save the maps required for your journey before setting off, while still connected to Wi-Fi. Then the maps can be used later *offline*, i.e. without an Internet connection.

Enter the name of your destination into Google Maps. Use two fingers to pinch or stretch the required area for your journey. Tap the 3-bar menu button at the top left of the screen and shown at the top of page 171 and select **Offline areas**. Then tap the blue button shown on the right. The **Download this area?** window appears as shown below, then tap **DOWNLOAD** at the bottom right.

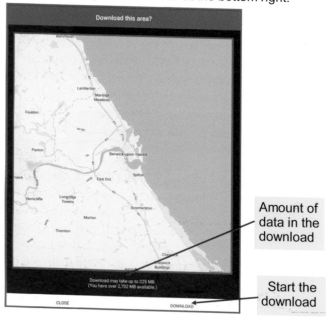

Amount of data in the download

Start the download

Enter a name for the offline area and then tap **SAVE**. This area will then be available for use offline on a journey, after selecting **Offline areas** from the Google Maps 3-bar menu.

Scanning QR Codes

An Android smartphone or tablet can be used to scan the latest form of bar code, known as the *QR* (*Quick Response*) code. As shown below, this consists of a matrix of squares of different sizes. The QR code can be used to represent several thousand numerical and text characters. There are several free apps in the Play Store for scanning bar codes.

QR codes frequently appear in advertisements and publications. The example below appears in the user guide for the HP Deskjet 2540.

Scan to learn about your printer.
www.hp.com/eu/m/dj2540
Standard data rates may apply. Might not be available in all languages.

When you scan a QR code, in this example a link appears to a Web site belonging to the company or organisation. This is far quicker than typing in the URL (i.e. Web address), even if you happen to know it. In an advertisement, if only the Web address is given, you probably won't bother to write it down or remember it. Without the QR code scanner, you are likely to ignore or forget an advertiser's Web site.

The links to the Web sites are stored in the **History** of the QR code scanner app and can therefore be used later at any time.

QR codes are also used to store bank and credit card information and to manage payments.

Several QR and barcode scanner apps are available in the Play Store, such as the one shown on the right. These can be downloaded and installed as described in Chapter 3.

QR & Barcode Scanner
Gamma Play .com
4.3 ★

To start scanning, tap the scanner icon on the Apps screen, as shown on the right below. The scanning screen opens with four right-angled guide lines as shown in blue below. Keep holding the smartphone or tablet with the guide lines framing the QR code.

Scan to learn about your printer.
www.hp.com/eu/m/dj2540
Standard data rates may apply. Might not be available in all languages.

You may hear a beep before a link to a Web site appears. Alternatively, the **Scan** window shown below on the left is displayed, with a *link* to **Open** the Web site and a button to **Share** the link using Dropbox, Google Drive, etc. In this example, the HP Help Web site opens as shown below on the right.

Index